AMERICAN HERITAGE

February, 1974 · Volume XXV, Number 2

American Heritage has been selected by the Library of Congress for reproduction on recordings called "Talking Books," distributed free by regional libraries in the United States to those unable to use conventional print because of a visual or physical handicap. For information write the Library of Congress, Division for the Blind and Physically Handicapped, 1291 Taylor Street, N.W., Washington, D.C. 20542.

JOHN F. URWILLER

LETTER FROM THE EDITOR

Every man, we are told, craves some distinction, and we have ours, a plain, simple, and unfortunately secure one. We come from the least beautiful town in New England—New London, Connecticut, known to sportswriters as the Whaling City but to those who operate on less historical principles as Eyesore-on-Sea. Our citizens have been celebrated in the past as smugglers, as embezzlers, as book burners; our town as a nest of privateers, a rendezvous for rumrunners, a Navy "liberty" port, and the watering place of the hard-drinking family of the late Eugene O'Neill. Several of his plays deal with our declining fortunes. Now we are in the papers again, because our city fathers are about to tear down our railroad station, a registered national landmark designed in 1885 by one of the great American architects, H. H. Richardson.

Any distinction, of course, must be earned, and New London did not attain its lack of beauty by an act of God, like Sodom or Gomorrah, or by inheritance, as did such mill towns as Lawrence, Massachusetts, and Bridgeport. We worked to get where we are. Our city stands upon one of the most beautiful harbors in the world, the mouth of what geologists call a drowned river, the Thames, wide, deep, and locally mispronounced to rhyme with "James." (We sound the h, too.) Despite these advantages it was already mean and unsightly by the time of the Revolution, according to our able local historian, Miss Frances Caulkins. During the war we were given a second chance when Benedict Arnold, a native of New London County and by then a British general, came with a British force in 1781, took the town, and burned it to the ground, perhaps on purpose, perhaps not. Our tiny garrison fired one round and fled across the river.

We missed the chance provided by this native son. As Miss Caulkins tells us, we rebuilt an even more unsightly town, for partial evidence of which she cites the story of an early steamboat heading into our once busy harbor. A stranger was standing next to the captain, who heard him say, "If I only had the money!" The captain turned and asked, "What would you do if you only had the money?" "Buy that town and burn it," said the stranger.

Miss Caulkins, who would feel at home in New London today, died more than a century ago at the height of the whaling boom, in the 1850's and 60's, when the city had only one less ship at sea than New Bedford and when the streets began to be lined with the imposing columned mansions of the shipowners and the smaller but picturesque houses and cabins of the masters and crews. After whaling waned, the New York Yacht Club discovered the lower harbor of New London, and a string of enormous summer "cottages" of the Newport variety went up along the drive on the shore to house the rich in their migrations. But New London's destructive spirit asserted itself, aided to be sure by the Depression. The great houses are gone, along with the yachts, the rambling summer hotels, and the Yale-Harvard regatta. Street widening took away the trees, which obscured the fire-sale signs of the merchants. Urban renewal in its most acute form levelled most of the old captains' cabins and most of the mansions, which had become offices and funeral parlors or slums, so that the center of town looks like Carthage after the Romans were through with it. Large areas lie empty, gone to weeds and beer cans, pierced by streets that go nowhere; and the rest is full of neomodern housing, landscaped in trash and decorated with bas-relief graffiti. (This is from bas, meaning "low," and relief, signifying "financed by welfare.")

Practically all we have left in the center of the town, besides a few churches and one building that escaped Arnold (but is now stuccoed over and falling to ruin), is a line of four fine old Greek Revival mansions called Whale Oil Row. One of them was badly burned recently but is being entirely restored by a public-spirited doctor. Across the street, where once stood a replica of Mount Vernon, is a full-grown A & P. At the head of the main shopping street stands a handsome Georgian wooden clapboard courthouse, built in 1784, we believe, that has often been threatened as obsolete by generations of local politicians but by oversight not yet actually destroyed. At the foot of the same street, now being converted into an automobile-free shopping mall called Captain's Walk, one looks along the brand-new but, alas, fake cobblestones to Richardson's massive three-story red brick Union Station.

It is called Union because it handled several railroads: the Central Vermont Railroad trains to Brattleboro and, until the wholesale cutbacks that gave us Amtrak, the passenger line to Norwich and Worcester. Principally it handled passengers and freight for the shore line of the New Haven Railroad—now swallowed by Penn Central—from Boston to New York. It is still a very busy and imposing place, if unspeakably dirty and decrepit. Amtrak would like to save it, but New London's standing order doesn't care about that. The big old building crosses the bottom of our town's main street like the top of a T, cutting off part of the view of the docks, the harbor, and the town of Groton across the Thames. The chief local argument is that it must come down because it is so dirty, as though cleaning had never been invented. The second argument is that it spoils the view, which will only impress those who have never seen the full vista of downtown Groton. The third is a xenophobic attack on "meddling outsiders," which is, considering the ever-changing ethnic cast of New London, too preposterous to discuss.

But if the arguments are weak, the bulldozers of New London are strong. They will raze that station somehow, and they will get us the squattest, flimsiest, most modernistic glass-and-plastic passenger shed cum bar and grill between Bridgeport and Boston, with a fine view of the submarine works across the river, the garbage floating around the docks, and any British expeditionary force that may happen in, some day, to give us another chance.

—Oliver Jensen

AMERICAN HERITAGE

The Magazine of History

EDITOR
Oliver Jensen

ARTICLES EDITOR: E. M. Halliday
EXECUTIVE EDITOR: Nat Brandt
ASSOCIATE EDITOR: Barbara Klaw
ART DIRECTOR: Emma Landau
ASSISTANT EDITOR: Richard F. Snow

PICTURE EDITORS
Carla Davidson   Mary Dawn Earley
ASSISTANT: Devorah K. Cohen

COPY EDITOR
Anne D. Steinhardt
ASSISTANT COPY EDITOR: Deborah Agrest

EDITORIAL ASSISTANTS
Anne Anderson   Caroline Jones

CONSULTING EDITORS
Joan Paterson Kerr   Allan L. Damon

CONTRIBUTING EDITORS
Robert C. Alberts   Robert S. Gallagher
Richard M. Ketchum Bernard A. Weisberger

ADVISORY BOARD
Carl Carmer   Eric F. Goldman
Gerald Carson   Louis C. Jones
Henry Steele Commager Alvin M. Josephy, Jr.
Marshall B. Davidson   Howard H. Peckham
John A. Garraty   Francis S. Ronalds
S. K. Stevens

AMERICAN HERITAGE PUBLISHING CO., INC.

PRESIDENT AND PUBLISHER
Paul Gottlieb

SENIOR EDITORS
Bruce Catton   Joseph J. Thorndike

EDITORIAL ART DIRECTOR
Murray Belsky

AMERICAN HERITAGE is published every two months by American Heritage Publishing Co., Inc.; editorial and executive offices, 1221 Ave. of the Americas, New York, N.Y. 10020. Treasurer, Marjorie C. Dyer; Secretary, John C. Taylor III. Correspondence about subscriptions should be sent to American Heritage Subscription Office, 383 West Center St., Marion, Ohio 43302. Single copies: $5. Annual subscriptions: $20 in U.S. and Canada; $21 elsewhere. A ten-year Index of Volumes VI–XV is available at $5; five-year Index of Volumes XVI–XX at $5.

AMERICAN HERITAGE considers but assumes no responsibility for unsolicited materials; these require return postage. Title registered U.S. Patent Office. Second-class postage paid at New York, N.Y., and at additional mailing offices.

Sponsored by
American Association for State & Local History · Society of American Historians

CONTENTS *February, 1974 · Volume XXV, Number 2*

COVER: This busy, hopeful scene is a detail from a famous painting by Edward Lamson Henry, painted in 1892—sixty-one years after the event itself. It hangs in the collection of the Albany Institute of History and Art. Some notes on the painting and the affair itself are given on page 97. The rug on our back cover, certainly the largest oriental (ten feet by over thirteen) on American patriotic themes, was ordered from Persian weavers to celebrate both George Washington's bicentenary and the Sesquicentennial Exposition of American independence in 1926. Since it arrived too late for the latter celebration, the present owners, Kent-Costikyan, Inc., of New York, are looking hopefully for someone who will acquire it for the Bicentennial—to hang on a wall, not, perish the thought, to walk on.

H.M.
STANLEY
1893

The Making of an
AMERICAN LION

*A Welsh waif adopted a new country and a
new name and then became—thanks to a New York newspaper—
the most famous African explorer of his time*

By TIMOTHY SEVERIN

On Sunday, December 8, 1872, the manager of the Theatre Comique on Broadway took the unusual step of buying up almost the entire front page of the New York *Herald* to puff the triumph of his latest presentation. It was called *Africa or Livingstone and Stanley,* and, to judge from the ecstatic reviews that were quoted, the show was a ringing success. The popular comedy team of Harrigan and Hart had been lured away from their previous engagement at a rival theatre in order to play the leads, and as the Comique was making an all-out attempt to broaden its audience appeal, the *Herald*'s lady readers were particularly assured that the theatre and its program offered an enjoyable evening that no well-bred lady need shun.

The theme of the entertainment was, of course, the spectacular rescue of Dr. David Livingstone in Central Africa by Henry Morton Stanley, though the tale had been enlivened by such extra stage characters as "the Congo Dancers of the Land of Crocodiles" and a cast-away Irish lady, Mrs. Biddy Malone, who in Scene VIII taught the Africans an Irish war cry. The *pièce de résistance* of this light-hearted farrago was, to the delight of the audience, the inevitable tableau as Stanley strode on stage in his African kit with an enormous Stars and Stripes to discover a wilting Livingstone at his last gasp. Raising his hat, Stanley uttered the immortal phrase "Doctor Livingstone, I presume," a remark that sent the Comique's audience into guffaws of delight.

It was no accident that the *Herald* had been chosen as the vehicle for the Comique's advertising. The *Herald* was the most popular paper in New York. It was at the height of its power and flamboyance; its theatre reviews were crisply written and widely read, and its advertising carried enormous impact. People turned instinctively to the *Herald* for everything that was racy, gossipy, and entertaining. Above all, it was the newspaper that had "made" Stanley. It was the *Herald,* in the person of its eccentric millionaire-editor, James Gordon Bennett, Jr., that had sent Stanley into Africa as its special correspondent to look for Livingstone. The *Herald* had paid all Stanley's bills, and it was the *Herald* that had consistently carried as journalistic scoops all of Stanley's dis-

patches. Indeed, Stanley's last cable summarizing his exploits was so lengthy that it cost two thousand dollars to send, a sum that Bennett considered well spent if it helped to reassert the *Herald*'s dominance over all its rival New York papers.

What Bennett and the *Herald* succeeded in doing in 1872 was to create for the American public that rare creature, *Leo Africanus Americanus,* an African lion from America. Naturally there had been plenty of other African lions before, men like Richard Francis Burton and John Hanning Speke, who had searched for the source of the Nile, and Livingstone himself. But they had all been uncompromisingly British. Stanley, by contrast, was presented by the *Herald* as an American through and through, a bluff, no-nonsense traveler from the New World who had trod boldly into the heart of Africa, beaten the English at their own game, and carried off the greatest prize in African exploration. In the words of the official citation from Mayor A. Oakey Hall of New York, Stanley was a "young journalist who took the commission of a New York newspaper in his pocket and the

Henry Morton Stanley's many years of exploration were behind him when he was painted in 1893 by his wife, Dorothy Tennant, a talented English artist. Although the pose was heroic, the fifty-two-year-old Stanley was a sick man, suffering from chronic gastritis and malaria.

American flag in his hand and so started to find a British explorer who had been practically abandoned by his own government in the wilds of Central Africa. . . ."

The man at the center of this enthusiasm was not, at first sight, obvious timber to turn into a public hero. Thirty-one years old, Stanley cut a rather squat and graceless figure. His arms and legs seemed too short for his thick, powerful body, and his rather rubicund face was chiefly remarkable for its air of determined pugnacity. His hair, once black, had turned a pepper-and-salt color during his African trek, and he behaved with an awkward combination of bluntness and shyness. Queen Victoria, who had met him two months previously, described him as "a determined, ugly little man—with a strong American twang." When excited he could get carried away, gesticulate wildly, and blurt out all manner of indiscreet remarks, yet at the same time it was common knowledge that he himself took offense easily. Thus the *Herald*'s successful publicity campaign to boost Stanley into the headlines was a considerable feat.

Stanley returned to New York from his Livingstone trip aboard the *Cuba* from Liverpool on November 20, 1872, a year and ten days after his memorable encounter with Livingstone. As usual the *Cuba*'s arrival was reported by one of the *Herald*'s fast patrol boats that constantly cruised off the port, waiting to pick up advance shipping news ahead of the rival press.

But as she entered the Narrows the *Cuba* was also greeted by the *Fletcher*, a steam vessel specially chartered by a group of Stanley's friends and newspaper associates. From the *Fletcher*'s mast streamed an enormous red pennant on which was written the words "welcome home Henry Stanley," and from her decks a crowd of Stanley's admirers and members of the American Geographical Society waved and cheered. Stanley was whisked away by carriage from the docks to the *Herald*'s office, where he had an interview with his boss, Bennett, and was applauded by his colleagues.

The next day a *Herald* reporter was sent up to the Fifth Avenue Hotel, where Stanley was staying, with particular instructions to take a closer look at Kalulu, the small black boy whom Stanley had brought back with him from Africa and who was already something of a showman. The *Herald*'s reporter found Kalulu prancing about dressed up as Buttons in a page-boy suit, and there followed a hilariously garbled interview in alleged Swahili during which Kalulu cheerfully dropped on all fours to imitate a Moslem at prayer, sang a Swahili song, and only lost interest in the proceedings when he turned up some chestnuts to eat. Stanley himself was under siege from numerous callers who had come to offer their congratulations and were being rewarded with a glimpse of the trophies that the explorer had already picked up on his way through London. The chief of

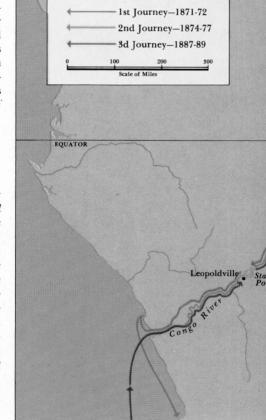

BOTH MAPS: FRANCIS & SHAW

1st Journey—1871-72
2nd Journey—1874-77
3d Journey—1887-89

0   100   200   300
Scale of Miles

EQUATOR

Leopoldville   Sta
                Po
Congo River

Three of Stanley's most memorable treks into the heart of what he called Darkest Africa: The blue line traces his successful search for Livingstone, whom he found at Ujiji and with whom he explored the north end of Lake Tanganyika. The green line follows Stanley's peril-filled exploration of the Congo River, a feat that took almost three years to complete and resulted in the famed explorer's name being attached to seven cataracts of the upper Congo (Stanley Falls), a nearby town (Stanleyville), and, well over a thousand miles away, a broad expanse of the river (Stanley Pool). Like the search for Livingstone, this journey began at Zanzibar and headed westward across Central Africa. Upon reaching the Atlantic Ocean, Stanley and his men boarded a ship for the return to Zanzibar, via the Cape of Good Hope. The third trek, undertaken to rescue Emin Pasha, the beleaguered governor of the equatorial province, from rebel Sudanese, is marked by the red line. On this trip, Stanley left Zanzibar by ship, rounded the Cape, and travelled inland from the mouth of the Congo. He found Emin at the southern edge of Lake Albert and together they headed eastward to the coast and thence to Zanzibar. Our map employs the place names of that time.

The historic meeting of Stanley and Livingstone at Ujiji on November 10, 1871, was devoid of any display of emotion, though nearly a year had passed since Stanley landed in Africa to begin his search. "It was the dignity that a white man and leader of an expedition ought to possess," he said, "that prevented me from running to shake hands with the venerable traveller...it was very tempting."

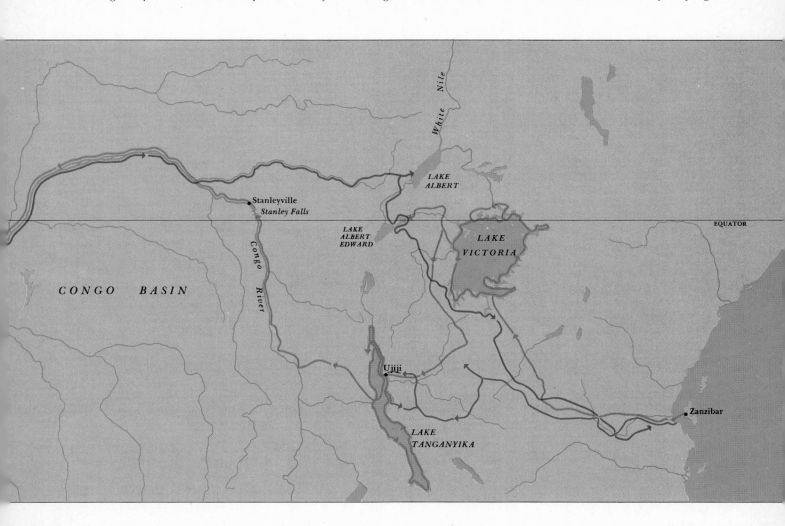

these prizes was a splendid gold snuff-box sent to him by Queen Victoria. The lid was decorated with a blue and white enamel background on which appeared the devices of rose, thistle, and shamrock worked in precious stones. In the center of this arrangement was set the Queen's personal monogram, V.R., surrounded by an imperial crown. Both the crown and the initials were also picked out in diamonds. Opening the lid one read on the reverse side the inscription

Presented by
HER MAJESTY, QUEEN VICTORIA
to
HENRY MORTON STANLEY, ESQ.
in recognition of the prudence and zeal
displayed by him
in opening communication with
DOCTOR LIVINGSTONE
and thus relieving the general anxiety
felt in regard to the fate of
that distinguished Traveller.
London, August 17, 1872.

Two nights after his arrival Stanley attended a reception given in his honor by the Lotos Club. This club, which later changed its name to the more familiar spelling Lotus, was composed largely of newspapermen, merchants, and clerics, and their clubhouse at Irving Place was specially decorated for the occasion with, among other items, a large "welcome" wreath hung over the door. Stanley arrived punctually at eleven, a half hour after the main throng of guests had assembled to cheer him. As usual, Stanley thanked his hosts for their hospitality and stressed his delight on coming home to the United States. He raised a few laughs by recounting how he had discomfited the English. Whitelaw Reid, the president of the Lotos and editor of the rival *Tribune,* then eulogized at length on Stanley's achievement as an American journalist; and, as the evening grew more convivial, various other speakers jumped up to add their own notions, usually with bad jokes and worse puns, one being on the fact that Livingstone had seen African natives eating lotus roots.

So the lionization of Stanley gathered speed, ably controlled by the *Herald* and greatly enjoyed by New York. Over the weekend he and Kalulu visited Gurney's photographic galleries to have more than twenty portraits taken in various heroic poses, in African dress as well as in western clothing. Among the props Stanley kept by the fireplace at the Fifth Avenue Hotel was a breech-loading gun that, he claimed, Livingstone himself had used against hippopotamuses. Doctor Livingstone's brother, John, who had emigrated to Canada, also came down to New York to congratulate and thank the explorer, an arrival that the *Herald* greeted with the headline LIVINGSTONE FINDS STANLEY.

Not that everything was plain sailing for the returned hero. Stanley had brought back with him from Africa the seeds of a virulent illness, probably a combination of malaria and dysentery. This was to plague him for the rest of his life, and a bout of this illness laid him low on the evening he was scheduled to attend another gala reception, this time with the American Geographical Society in the Cooper Institute. Instead he was obliged to send a last-minute apology for his absence by the hand of John Livingstone, who stood in for him. Later that week, however, he made amends by attending the splendid banquet that the geographers gave for him at Delmonico's. Nearly two hundred people attended. Stanley was in great form, flourishing his prize snuffbox from Victoria and announcing that "it is peculiarly pleasant and gratifying to receive such honour as this from, as I may say, one's own kindred. It is not often a prophet is honoured in his own country, but I think, though I am not exactly a prophet, that at least a traveller can be recognised in his native land."

Naturally enough, an instant Stanley industry flared up in the wake of his success. Besides the *Africa* show there was a skit in another review that depicted the Royal Geographical Society's council in London as a conclave of doddering old savants who collapsed with shock when Stanley strode in on their committee meeting and announced that he had found Livingstone. A local humorist, Don Bryant, managed to attract New York audiences by giving spoof lectures in a pseudo-explorer style on the adven-

This decorative postcard commemorates the state dinner given Stanley in 1890 by King Leopold II of Belgium aboard the Prince Albert. It was highly unusual for a commoner (Stanley was not even knighted until 1899) to be accorded such an honor.
ROYAL GEOGRAPHICAL SOCIETY, LONDON

tures of an African who came to New Jersey to search for the source of the Somerset River. Meeting a native, he inquired "Brrzknokho rkndorok-ledklokulla," which—predictably—was translated as "Dr. Livingstone, I believe? My name is Stanley." Meanwhile a Philadelphia publisher quickly got together with a San Francisco accomplice to prepare a book that allegedly gave the full account of the Livingstone rescue. The book was enticingly dressed up in an engraved cover showing African animals surrounded by jungle foliage. In fact it was nothing but a hodgepodge stolen from Stanley's earlier published dispatches and padded out with imaginary African geography and zoology lifted from

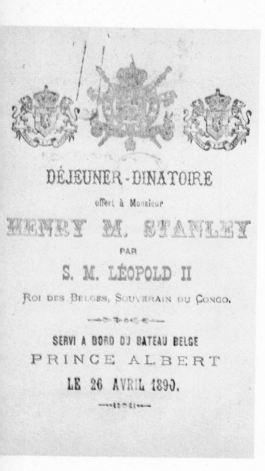

other African journals. There were also Stanley's photo portraits on sale, Stanley mementos, and Stanley jokes. The only other national figure to rival him was Jay Gould, arrested that same week for manipulating nearly ten million dollars' worth of Erie Railroad stock. And even here a touch of Stanley mania intervened. The *Herald* reporter hotfooted down to Wall Street to interview the notorious financier, caught sight of his prey in the Street, and, so the report alleged, intercepted his man by going boldly up to him and asking "Mr. Gould, I presume?"

But as with other overnight heroes, the yeast of excitement eventually turned sour for Stanley. The acclaim was simply too much to sustain, and heady indulgence brought its usual retribution on the morning after. Stanley's nemesis was the series of African lectures that had been booked in advance by a quicksilver impresario at the allegedly enormous sum of thirty thousand dollars. A successful lecture series would have won for him

the final acme of public approval (Harriet Beecher Stowe was speaking that same month at the Y.M.C.A.), and Stanley was due to appear at the prestigious Steinway Hall. Tickets were offered at the steep price of ten dollars for eight lectures or—as the first night approached—at one dollar per performance. Carried away with his commercial prospects, the promoter oversold his program badly. Advertising in the papers, he claimed that Stanley's topics would include LIFE IN CENTRAL AFRICA; THE HORRORS OF THE SLAVE TRADE; TRIUMPHS OF CHRISTIANITY IN THE FABULOUS LAND; MARCH OF THE HERALD EXPEDITION INTO THE LAND OF THE MOON; THE BATTLE OF THE JUNGLE; TRIBUTE TO THE KING OF UBBA; LIVINGSTONE'S MISSIONARY AND SCIENTIFIC WORK; THE CAVERNS OF TANGANYIKA; THE DISCOVERY OF DOCTOR LIVINGSTONE; DOCTOR LIVINGSTONE'S STORY; MARCH TO NYASSA LAKE AND THE FAMOUS CAZEME; THE TREASURES OF THE WONDERFUL LAND; THE MYSTIC NILE AND ITS SOURCES, etc., etc. Shrewd critics might have pointed out that it all sounded too much like P. T. Barnum's advertisement in the next column, which announced "Dwarfs, Giants and Nondescripts" [in] his Great Hippodrome, along with "Colonel Routh Goshen the Largest Human Being in the Known World. Admiral Dot, Twenty Five Inches High" and a "Madagascar Family of Albinoes, and Wax Figures without Number. . . ."

Stanley's inaugural lecture was a near-fiasco. It started out well enough with the podium evocatively decorated with African shields and spears, the Stars and Stripes that Stanley had carried at the head of his caravan, a huge map of Africa, and the impish Kalulu. But Stanley himself was a flop; he droned on monotonously, his text was dry and poorly organized, there were too many long and incomprehensible African place names in it, and people at the back of the hall could not hear him.

The second lecture of the series was even worse. The audience was noticeably smaller, and the long-suffering reporter from the *Herald* who had been kind enough about the first effort could stand the tedium no longer. "Mr. Stanley," he snarled in his re-

view, "has utterly mistaken the necessities of the platform. His map of Central Africa is not used, and the specimens of cloths which he brings on the stage are quite useless, for he does not know how to make his hearers interested in them by making them illustrative of his subject. . . . he overlooks the personal and the peculiar, and treats only of the geographical and commonplace. . . . All this is unnecessary, and it would be cruel to Mr. Stanley not to say so."

Of course the cruelty was in being so caustic. Chastened, Stanley threw in his hand. The remainder of his lecture series was discreetly cancelled—so discreetly, indeed, that some thirty people showed up at Steinway Hall the following session and were surprised to find the building locked and in darkness. ". . . After repeated knocking," the New York *World* reported, "the janitor appeared to tell them that Stanley would not be appearing any more in the Hall owing to the fact that the former receipts of the lectures delivered did not meet expenses." The *World,* which had been looking for just this opportunity, gleefully published Stanley's discomfiture on its front page, and the Steinway management hastily arranged a substitute program of vocalists and piano with gallery seats for as little as twenty-five cents.

The lecture failure was only one of Stanley's disasters. While he was in the full flush of popularity, Horace Greeley died and the papers were swamped with his obituaries. In particular the *Tribune,* usually reliable for a contest with the *Herald,* went in heavily for memorabilia about the late Presidential candidate who, after all, had helped to found the newspaper. Then the Fifth Avenue Hotel burned down, and there was not even mention of whether Stanley had moved out beforehand or how he had escaped the blaze, which killed several of the maids. Typically, Bennett seized this chance to splash on his front page the new "Bennett building" currently under construction and supposedly

The intrepid explorer and his African "boy" Kalulu were photographed in front of a mock jungle scene in a London studio after his return from finding Livingstone in 1872.

fireproof. Moreover, Christmas was due, and so *Africa* came off the boards at the Comique, and a pantomime was put on in its place. By the end of the holidays almost the only scrap thrown Stanley's way was a puff for his book *How I Found Livingstone,* which was put on the list of recommended holiday reading. Thus in April, when Stanley left New York and sailed for his next journalistic assignment, his departure was scarcely noted.

Over the next eighteen years Stanley's career was to be an astonishing series of coups. Returning to central Africa in 1874, he was to make a masterly trek lasting more than a thousand days. It took him clear across the middle belt of the continent and solved two of the foremost problems of African geography, namely, the extent of Lake Victoria relative to the Nile and the course of the Congo River.

The Congo voyage itself was a great adventure. Travelling in a forty-foot open boat of Stanley's own design—it could be dismantled and carried in sections overland—the explorer floated, blustered, and fought his way down the length of the previously unknown waterway. Of his three white companions two died of fever, and the third was drowned in the Congo's rapids. Sharp battles were fought against river tribes who attacked the strangers with squadrons of war canoes, and conditions eventually became so treacherous that the Zanzibari coxswain went mad and rushed off into the jungle shrieking "The sea! the sea!" Yet scarcely had Stanley emerged from this ordeal when he plunged back into Africa, this time at the request of King Leopold of Belgium, to develop the enormous Congo basin. Stanley's campaign was of Pharaonic proportions. Commanding a small army of white volunteers and Zanzibari porters, he built a roadway around the worst cataracts, dragged steamers overland to launch them on Stanley Pool, as the inland lake of the Congo was called in his honor, and laid the foundations of the Congo Free State.

But these remarkable achievements were still in the future when Americans were casting a critical eye over the brand-new African lion presented to them so glibly by the New York *Herald* in 1872. Indeed, the people of the United States had earned themselves the privilege of treating Stanley exactly as they wished—handsomely, shabbily, or not at all—for the fact was that Stanley owed a tremendous debt to his country of adoption. He derived from the United States not only his initial fame for the Livingstone rescue but also to a large degree his self-confidence, his education, and what *savoir-faire* he had. In many ways his life was the American dream come true, and it was by a quirk of history that he achieved renown in an African, rather than an American, context.

Stanley's original name had been John Rowlands, and he was the illegitimate son of a Welsh girl who had promptly handed the infant over to the care of his grandfather living in the small Welsh town of Denbigh. There he was looked after until he was six years old, when, on the pretext that he was being taken on a visit to his Aunt Mary, he was walked down to the local workhouse and callously handed over to the workmaster, to be held in his custody until placed in suitable (and probably menial) employment. Stanley's life in the workhouse was a nightmare. Like the other inmates he was wretchedly fed and clothed, forced to work in freezing conditions, and savagely tormented. The chief culprit in this Oliver Twist existence was the workmaster, a crippled brute of a man who had lost a hand in a mining accident, been put out to pasture in his present job, and took out his malice on his wards. Later he was found to be certifiably insane. At fifteen, according to his memoirs, Stanley got into a fight with the workmaster, knocked him down, and fled from the workhouse before his tormentor regained consciousness. Briskly handed on from one relative to the next, Stanley finally obtained a job as a cabin boy aboard the American packet ship *Windermere,* sailing from Liverpool to New Orleans.

It was not a happy introduction to Americans, because the Yankee packets were notoriously hard driven, and the youthful Welshman was swindled and mistreated. He signed on as a cabin boy, but it was an old trick whereby the moment the vessel put to sea, the "cabin boy" was kicked forward to take his place with the regular sailors and had to serve his passage as a cut-price deck hand. Similarly, it was common practice to haze the newcomer so badly toward the end of the trip that the victim jumped ship at the first port without collecting his wages, which were pocketed by the captain. Certainly the technique worked well with the Welsh truant. At New Orleans Stanley scurried off the packet ship and, after spending one night bedded down among the cotton bales on the levee, headed into the city to look for work.

It was at this time that he had what can best be described as one of those tremendous strokes of good luck based on coincidence that were to propel him to fame. Trudging up Tchapitoulas Street early in the morning, past the commercial houses and stores, he saw a middle-aged man, prosperously dressed in a dark alpaca suit and tall hat, seated outside No. 3 store, the premises of Speake and McCreary, wholesale and commission merchants. Judging by the man's appearance and the way his chair was tilted languidly back against the stone porch, Stanley mistook him for the proprietor and, walking over, blurted out, "Do you want a boy, sir?" "Eh?" the man replied with a start. "What did you say?" "I want some work, sir," answered Stanley. "I asked if you wanted a boy."

The stranger so casually approached was to alter the future explorer's life profoundly. The man's name was Henry Stanley, and he made a comfortable living as a commission agent, selling hardware and general goods to cotton planters and merchants along the Mississippi and Arkansas rivers.

travelling minister, made the sign of the cross on the lad's forehead and baptized him. It was only then that Stanley learned how the commission agent had always wanted to adopt a boy and had even visited the local orphanage in search of one. So that the words of the young runaway suddenly approaching him in the street with "Do you want a boy, sir?" had voiced his inner feelings.

His protégé's gratitude was boundless. The former John Rowlands, waif, took his benefactor's name, listened to every word his mentor spoke, com-

was almost inconsolable.

But Stanley had very much more than an emotional attachment to America through his foster father. His African training also really began at New Orleans. He was taken on as an assistant at Speake and McCreary's store, and it was here and upriver that he developed his remarkable flair for organization and detail that was later to characterize his expeditions. At his prime in Africa, Stanley the explorer was capable of handling vast amounts of men and materials. It was nothing for him to control a marching column

"*They are heroes, these poor ignorant children of Africa . . .*" Stanley said of his men after their astounding exploits in exploring the Congo River. "*They had rallied to my voice like veterans; and in the hour of need they had never failed me.*" He sits above with his stalwart retinue upon completion of their return trip by ship to Zanzibar in 1877. Three white companions had died on the three-year-long expedition.

The Autobiography of Sir Henry Morton Stanley, 1909

Not only did he help provide the young Welsh immigrant with his first decent job, but he also befriended him, educated him, arranged his commercial training, eradicated the boy's singsong Welsh accent, and finally adopted the waif. This adoption took place soon after the death of the commission agent's wife and was a curious little ceremony in which Stanley senior, who turned out to have once been a

piled a log book of his advice, and even went so far as to adopt his style of handwriting. The first time that young Stanley received a letter from his foster father, he noted the signature and copied it for his own, retaining the distinctive flourish that was to appear on all Stanley's later correspondence. When Mr. Stanley senior died of yellow fever on a business trip to Cuba in 1861, the future African explorer

of porters three-quarters of a mile long and directed by bugle calls; and on the Congo he was to supervise the operation of an entire fleet of steamers carrying an army of natives with all their stores and munitions deep into the heart of the continent. All this was foreshadowed in his apprenticeship as a Mississippi commission agent: the bags and bales, the lists of lading, the best ways of packaging, all the exper-

CONTINUED ON PAGE 82

VETO

> **ve·to** (vē'tō) *n., pl.* **-toes. 1.** The vested power or constitutional right of one branch or department of government, especially the right of a chief executive, to reject a bill passed by a legislative body and thus prevent or delay its enactment into law. **2.** The exercise of this right. **3.** The official document communicating the rejection and the reasons for it. Also called "veto message." **4.** Any authoritative prohibition or rejection of a proposed or intended act. —*tr.v.* **vetoed, -toing, -toes. 1.** To prevent (a legislative bill) from becoming law by exercising the power of veto. **2.** To forbid or prevent authoritatively; prohibit. [Latin *vetō*, I forbid, from *vetāre†*, to forbid.] —**ve'to'er** *n.*

—The American Heritage Dictionary

By ALLAN L. DAMON

The veto is without question the most powerful single weapon available to the President under the Constitution. It places him squarely in the center of the lawmaking process, on an equal footing with Congress, and by its very existence guarantees that the separation of powers at the heart of American government will not, in Hamilton's phrase, be based on "mere parchment . . . boundaries." All things considered, it is a remarkable power for an executive to wield in a republican state.

What is perhaps most remarkable about the veto is that it should exist at all, for the colonial experience with strong executive rule had not been good. But the delegates to the Constitutional Convention in 1787 were determined to create a balanced government in which power would be divided by function and not concentrated in any one branch. They understood that to make such a system work they must equip each component part with, as Hamilton wrote, "a constitutional and effectual power of self defence." As they ransacked the past for models they reluctantly concluded that for the President this meant the veto, a power that traces back to ancient times, to Sparta and to Rome. Conscious that it was clearly open to abuse, they nonetheless settled on it, again in Hamilton's words, as "a shield to the executive" to blunt the great powers they had given the Senate and the House and as "a salutary check" on Congress to prevent the "passing of bad laws, through haste, inadvertence, or design."

What the Founding Fathers created was, in fact, two vetoes, one qualified and the other absolute. As provided for in Section 7, Article 1 of the Constitution (where, by the way, the word "veto" does not appear), the President must approve or disapprove any bill or joint resolution that has passed both houses of Congress. If he signs the bill, it is law. If he does not sign it and Congress remains in session, the bill becomes law without his signature after ten days, Sundays excepted. If, however, the President disapproves the bill, he may exercise the qualified, or regular, veto when Congress is still in session by returning the unsigned bill within the ten-day period to the house where it originated, along with his objections to it. If two thirds of the members of that house present and voting agree to override the veto, the bill then passes to the other house. If two thirds of the members present and voting there also agree to override, the bill becomes a law. Should either house fail to muster a two-thirds vote, the President's veto is sustained, and the bill is dead.

The pocket veto, by contrast, is absolute. It is exercised only when Congress has gone out of session for longer than ten days or is in formal adjournment at the end of its term. Under such circumstances the President's veto is final because the rejected bill cannot be returned to Congress for further action, and the veto cannot be overridden.

Despite the Founding Fathers' fears that this great power would be subject to abuse and a potential source of tyranny, the veto has had a remarkably placid history. Since 1787 it has become nationally accepted as an important—if not essential—part of the system of checks and balances. It has been subjected to few challenges in the courts and then, usually, only to clarify certain technicalities. For example, must a constitutional amendment be submitted to the President for his approval before it is sent on to the states for their approval? The Supreme Court has twice ruled no.

Although Congress has occasionally considered constitutional amendments to weaken or eliminate the veto altogether (most notably in the aftermath of Jackson's Presidency), the only serious effort at changing the power has come from the Presidents themselves. Every chief executive since Grant has urged the passage of an amendment giving the President an item veto in appropriations bills, a power currently available to the governors of forty-three states. More than a hundred amendments to that effect have been introduced since 1875; all have died in committee. Thus the President must still approve or disapprove a bill in its entirety. He may not eliminate single items he believes to be inflationary or wasteful without rejecting the whole bill. Consequently every President since Franklin Roosevelt has impounded—that is, has refused to spend certain funds Congress has allocated [see "Impoundment," AMERICAN HERITAGE, December, 1973]. Congress, not unexpectedly, has often protested this practice, but its objections have not extended to the veto power itself, for unlike impoundment, which requires a broad reading of the Constitution and existing statutes, the veto authority and its limits are reasonably well defined in the Constitution. As a result, in the great majority of disputed vetoes the sources of controversy are the President's reasons for exercising the veto, not his generally acknowledged right to do so.

Moreover, as the record suggests, the veto has not been generally abused. In fact, its most powerful effect may well lie in the threat of its use rather than in its actual employment. Congress goes about its work conscious that the President is waiting in the wings to cast judgment on its efforts and—except in the most striking cases—tailors its compromises before, rather than after, a veto has been exercised, for again, as the record shows, the chances of an override are often slim indeed. The Presidents, in turn, have discovered, with some exceptions, that the impact of the veto is inversely related to the frequency of its use.

Finally it should be noted that the extension of the veto power beyond its narrowest limits has been a gradual affair. Nearly a dozen Presidents have contributed to its expansion over a hundred eighty-five years, while impoundment, for example, developed rapidly and dramatically in two administrations over thirty-three years. Where one has generated controversy, the other has produced little or none. Indeed, most commentators seem to accept the view of Lord Bryce, a nineteenth-century observer of American life, that the veto power "has worked wonderfully well."

Herewith some highlights and details:

● The veto currently exercised by the President of the United States remains unique among the powers granted to elected leaders of national states. Although the presidents of the Third and Fourth French Republics possessed a suspensive veto, it was never used.

● The monarch of Great Britain ostensibly may exercise a veto by withholding the royal assent (le roy le veult—"the king approves it"), but no monarch has done so since Queen Anne rejected a Scottish militia bill in March, 1707, using, as is customary, the Old French form la reyne s'avisera ("the queen will consider the matter"). Because the monarch is now expected to sign all bills at the direction of the cabinet and because all important bills are sent into Parliament by the ministers, or endorsed by them, the veto in all probability will never again be used. Were an unacceptable bill to be returned for the monarch's assent, the cabinet would either call for a new election to test its parliamentary strength or merely resign to make way for a new ministry.

● When the Constitution was drafted in 1787, the only existing executive veto in the United States—and the model the drafters eventually used—was in Massachusetts. Since then forty-nine states have granted their governors that power. (North Carolina is the exception.)

● Since 1789 congressmen have introduced nearly 941,000 separate bills and joint resolutions for possible enactment into law. The First Congress considered 144 measures and passed 118. At the present time an average of 22,000 new bills appear in each two-year term of Congress; most of them die quietly—and unmourned—in the labyrinths of congressional committees. Somewhere between 900 and 1,500 will eventually become law.

● Since the establishment of the government a hundred eighty-five years ago Congress has enacted nearly 86,000 laws. Some 40,500 originated as *public bills*, generally designed to affect the nation as a whole. Roughly 45,500, or more than half, began as *private bills*, designed to grant relief to specific individuals or groups named in the bill where the enforcement of other, existing statutes would work a hardship in taxation, immigration restrictions, military pensions, and the like.

● Thirty Presidents have cast a total of 2,289 vetoes (through November, 1973). This represents about 2.6 per cent of all legislation submitted to the President for approval. A total of 1,315 were *regular vetoes*; 974 were *pocket vetoes*.

● Congress has overridden only 78 regular vetoes. This accounts for 6 per cent of all regular vetoes cast, or 3.4 per cent of all vetoes. Virtually all overrides were in support of public bills.

● Roughly 60 per cent of all vetoes have been directed to private bills. Congress has rarely brought such vetoes to a floor vote.

● Four Presidents (Franklin Roosevelt, Cleveland, Truman, and Eisenhower) together account for 1,650 vetoes, or approximately 72 per cent of all vetoes cast. Thirty of these vetoes were overridden.

● Andrew Johnson had the most vetoes overridden: 15 of 21 regular vetoes. Harry Truman is next with 12 overrides out of 180 regular vetoes cast.

● Eleven Presidents were never overridden: Washington, Madison, Monroe, Jackson, Polk, Buchanan, Lincoln, McKinley, Harding, Kennedy, and Lyndon Johnson. Among them they cast a total of 60 regular vetoes.

● Seven Presidents did not exercise the veto: John Adams, Jefferson, John Quincy Adams, William Henry Harrison, Taylor, Fillmore, and Garfield. None of them apparently was opposed to the power in principle; the occasion for its use simply did not arise.

● Van Buren exercised the pocket veto only, and just once, against a bill that was technically defective because an officer of the House had failed to sign it.

● Three Presidents who cast regular vetoes did not exercise the pocket veto: Washington, Monroe, and Pierce.

1792. George Washington was the first President to use the veto. He exercised it twice and was not overridden on either occasion. The first was cast in April, 1792, against a bill reapportioning the House of Representatives in accordance with the census of 1790. Washington argued that the reapportionment was unconstitutional because it provided a greater number of representatives than the Constitution permitted. His second veto came nearly five years later, in February, 1797, when he rejected a proposed reduction of cavalry units in the United States Army on defense grounds (they were needed in the West) and for economic reasons (many among those to be dismissed had served only one third of their enlistment, and because they had each been paid an enlistment bounty, the nation would stand to lose a substantial sum). Four hundred seven bills became law during Washington's two terms.

1811. **James Madison was the second President to use the veto, the first to employ the pocket veto, the first to veto a private bill, and the second of eleven Presidents not to be overridden. He cast 5 regular vetoes and 2 pocket vetoes. A total of 899 laws were enacted during his two administrations. His use of the veto followed Washington's practice of measuring the constitutionality of the bills presented to him, a curious invasion of the Supreme Court's recently asserted function of judicial review which characterized most early vetoes and which, for some reason, went unchallenged. Two of Madison's regular vetoes were directed against private bills in 1811; one of these would have incorporated a church in Virginia (for tax purposes), and the other would have provided federal land for a Baptist church in Mississippi. Both of them, as Madison saw it, violated the First Amendment's separation of church and state. Madison directed the first pocket veto against a change in the naturalization laws in November, 1812, shortly after Congress adjourned.**

1830. Andrew Jackson was only the fourth President to exercise the veto (5 regular and 7 pocket), but he substantially changed the grounds for its use. Although he, too, observed the earlier practice of measuring a bill's conformity to the Constitution, he proudly boasted that most of the legislation he struck down was repugnant to him for personal and political reasons. Fully half of his vetoes were directed to internal improvements and four to fiscal and banking measures. Although he was never overridden, his vetoes contributed to strained relations between the White House and Congress and generated considerable political turmoil during his eight years in office.

Two of his vetoes have historic interest. The first, cast on May 27, 1830, was an open assault on Henry Clay's "American System," a program of federal aid based on regional needs designed to speed the development of the nation's resources and to establish sectional harmony by, in effect, trading off high tariffs protecting eastern manufacturers for good roads and canals in the agricultural South and West. The Maysville Road Bill, introduced by Clay, was to be a crucial test of the whole concept. Jackson's veto checked but did not completely stop the movement for national improvements and was hailed by supporters of States' rights as a significant curb on burgeoning federal power. Jackson argued that the road had local—not general—value and thus lay outside the domain of Congress; if such projects were to have any basis in law, then an amendment to the Constitution was required. Although Jackson himself continued to authorize funds for construction and spent an average $1.3 million annually in this area, his veto generally dampened congressional enthusiasm for projects not clearly national in scope.

Jackson's second important veto was directed against the Bank of the United States on July 10, 1832. An extraordinarily complex problem involving States'-rights philosophy, a variety of regional questions, economic theories, and political aspirations, the "bank question" became the central issue in the Presidential campaign of 1832; historically it has become the most puzzling act in Jackson's career and has led historians to a variety of interpretations about the nature of Jacksonian Democracy and of Jackson himself. Probably no other veto has been more thoroughly studied or had more immediate and long-range effects on the nation than this. (The only close competitors are Andrew Johnson's vetoes during Reconstruction.) While the reasons for Jackson's veto are clear enough in his message to Congress—he indicts monopoly and special privilege—their meaning and Jackson's motives remain a source of endless debate.

1845. **The first congressional override of a veto came on March 3, 1845, after John Tyler exercised the last of his 6 regular vetoes. Earlier Tyler had ordered the Navy Department to let contracts for the building of two revenue cutters. As the contractors with the winning bids set to work procuring materials, but before actual construction of the vessels had begun, Congress passed a bill prohibiting the purchase of any additional cutters without its consent. As Tyler read the bill, the wording seemed to suggest that the contracts he had let were now void, and he took this to be a violation of the Constitution's clause in protection of contract. Congress did not agree and overrode his veto by a vote of 41–1 in the Senate and 127–30 in the House. The ships were not built.**

1866. By the end of the Civil War, when Andrew Johnson assumed the Presidency, the White House and Congress had achieved a compatible relationship in regard to the veto power. There had been a total of 57 vetoes, exercised by ten of sixteen Presidents, and 6 overrides. In all some 11,000 laws had been enacted. Except for the national uproar that greeted Jackson's vetoes of the Maysville Road Bill and the rechartering of the Bank, most vetoes had been quietly cast, easily sustained, and, outside of Congress, generally ignored.

Once Johnson was in the White House, however, all of that changed, and the President and Congress became bitter antagonists. The constitutional prize at stake was the control of Reconstruction, but this alone does not explain the warlike quality of the power struggle that ensued. Certainly the national mood of disillusionment in the aftermath of the bloodiest war the nation has ever fought contributed to the bitterness, as did the reluctance of the South to admit ideological defeat. The assassination of Lincoln and the circumstances of Johnson's succession played a part, and Johnson's own personality and habits were factors, particularly when compared with those of Jackson, the only earlier President to take on Congress in a public duel with the veto and the override as weapons. Where Jackson could fight and win because he had a majority of the population backing his stand, Johnson from the outset lacked broad popular support.

He vetoed a total of 29 bills, nearly half of which were

major Reconstruction measures. In the end 15 of his 21 regular vetoes were overridden, giving him the dubious distinction of having more overrides than any other President in history. More important, the net result was that Reconstruction passed from executive to congressional control.

Among the vetoes overridden were the Civil Rights Act of 1866, which conferred citizenship upon the blacks (later ruled unconstitutional in 1883); the New Freedmen's Bureau Bill, which gave the bureau, already empowered to care for the freed slaves, certain judicial powers; the First Reconstruction Act of 1867, which divided the South into five military districts and established the conditions by which the Southern states would be restored to the Union; the Tenure of Office Act of 1867, which limited the President's removal powers and the violation of which by Johnson subsequently led to his impeachment; and the Judiciary Act of 1869, which fixed the number of Supreme Court justices at nine.

1878. Rutherford B. Hayes cast his first of 12 regular vetoes on February 28, 1878, and was promptly overridden. At issue was the Bland-Allison Bill, which required the Treasury to purchase a minimum of $2 million in silver each month. The bill had been introduced by free-silver advocates in the House and, though weakened in the Senate, played a key role in keeping the silver issue alive until the McKinley-Bryan campaign of 1896.

After this initial loss Hayes was not again overridden. In 1879 he established a precedent with his veto of an army appropriations bill, and later a general appropriations bill, on the ground that Congress had in both instances tacked on general legislation riders unconnected to the original provisions or intent of the bills. The riders would have repealed the Force Acts of 1865 and 1874, which gave the President authority to use federal troops to supervise congressional elections where fraud or intimidation of voters was feared. The riders' appearance in the appropriations bills seemed an unwarranted interference with the discretionary powers of the President and a challenge to the separation of executive and legislative authority. Hayes informed Congress that he had no intention of using troops during elections but that Congress had no right to limit the President's deployment of military forces where "such employment is necessary to enforce the Constitution and laws of the United States." In any case, if Congress wished to consider the issue, it should do so openly in a general legislative bill and not under cover of a rider. Congress sustained both vetoes but attempted similar tactics in three other appropriation measures. Hayes vetoed all three and was not overridden.

1885. When Grover Cleveland began his first administration, fourteen Presidents had cast 205 vetoes (118 regular, 87 pocket). In the next four years Cleveland easily doubled the total of all other Presidents with 414 vetoes (304 regular, 110 pocket). He was overridden only twice. He struck down 343 private relief and pension bills; the remainder were mostly construction projects of a limited kind: a bridge over the Arkansas River, for example, and a public road leading to a national cemetery in Corinth, Mississippi. In his second term, beginning in 1893, he added 170 vetoes (43 regular, 127 pocket) and was overridden five times. Ninety-eight of his vetoes in the second

CONTINUED ON PAGE 81

The Veto Record*	Regular veto	Pocket veto	Total vetoes	Over-ridden
WASHINGTON	2	—	2	—
J. ADAMS	—	—	—	—
JEFFERSON	—	—	—	—
MADISON	5	2	7	—
MONROE	1	—	1	—
J. Q. ADAMS	—	—	—	—
JACKSON	5	7	12	—
VAN BUREN	—	1	1	—
W. H. HARRISON	—	—	—	—
TYLER	6	3	9	1
POLK	2	1	3	—
TAYLOR	—	—	—	—
FILLMORE	—	—	—	—
PIERCE	9	—	9	5
BUCHANAN	4	3	7	—
LINCOLN	2	4	6	—
A. JOHNSON	21	8	29	15
GRANT	45	49	94	4
HAYES	12	1	13	1
GARFIELD	—	—	—	—
ARTHUR	4	8	12	1
CLEVELAND, first term	304	110	414	2
B. HARRISON	19	25	44	1
CLEVELAND, second term	42	128	170	5
McKINLEY	6	36	42	—
T. ROOSEVELT	42	40	82	1
TAFT	30	9	39	1
WILSON	33	11	44	6
HARDING	5	1	6	—
COOLIDGE	20	30	50	4
HOOVER	21	16	37	3
F. ROOSEVELT	372	263	635	9
TRUMAN	180	70	250	12
EISENHOWER	73	108	181	2
KENNEDY	12	9	21	—
L. JOHNSON	16	14	30	—
NIXON **	22	17	39	5
	1,315	974	2,289	78

* Source: U.S. Congress, Senate Library, *Presidential Vetoes . . . 1789–1968; Statistical Abstract . . . 1972*
**As of November, 1973

"*I was arrested, of course ...*"

By ROBERT S. GALLAGHER

American women won the right to vote in 1920 largely through the controversial efforts of a young Quaker named Alice Paul. She was born in Moorestown, New Jersey, on January 11, 1885, seven years after the woman-suffrage amendment was first introduced in Congress. Over the years the so-called Susan B. Anthony amendment had received sporadic attention from the national legislators, but from 1896 until Miss Paul's dramatic arrival in Washington in 1912 the amendment had never been reported out of committee and was considered moribund. As the Congressional Committee chairman of the National American Woman Suffrage Association, Miss Paul greeted incoming President Woodrow Wilson with a spectacular parade down Pennsylvania Avenue. Congress soon began debating the suffrage amendment again. For the next seven years—a tumultuous period of demonstrations, picketing, politicking, street violence, beatings, jailings, and hunger strikes—Miss Paul led a determined band of suffragists in the confrontation tactics she had learned from the militant British feminist Mrs. Emmeline Pankhurst. This unrelenting pressure on the Wilson administration finally paid off in 1918, when an embattled President Wilson reversed his position and declared that woman suffrage was an urgently needed "war measure."

The woman who, despite her modest disclaimers, is accorded major credit for adding the Nineteenth Amendment to the Constitution is a 1905 graduate of Swarthmore College. She received her master's degree (1907) and her Ph.D. (1912) from the University of Pennsylvania. Miss Paul combined her graduate studies in 1908 and 1909 at the London School of Economics with volunteer work for the British suffrage movement. Together with another American activist, Lucy Burns, she was jailed several times in England and Scotland and returned to this country in 1910 with a reputation as an energetic and resourceful worker for women's rights. She promptly enlisted in the American suffrage movement, and opponents and friends alike soon were—and still are—impressed by her unflinching fearlessness. "Alice Paul is tiny and her hair has turned gray," a sympathetic feminist writer recently observed, "but she is not a sweet little gray-haired lady."

Miss Paul's single-minded devotion to The Cause is, of course,

Alice Paul at her Connecticut hearthside in 1972. The novel is misleading: she still reads little not clearly relevant to feminism.

DANIEL KRAMER

legendary in the women's movement. During the early struggle in the 1920's for the equal-rights amendment (E.R.A.) now up for ratification, she went back to college and earned three law degrees "because I thought I could be more useful to the campaign if I knew more about the law." A similar pragmatism continues to govern Miss Paul's daily activities. She admits to a gracious impatience with interviewers who seem, from her perspective, obsessed with the past. "Why in the world," she politely but firmly inquires, "would anyone want to know about that?" And she pointedly delayed her conversation with AMERICAN HERITAGE until after the 1972 Presidential election so that she could spend all her time getting the candidates publicly committed to the ratification of E.R.A. President Nixon, she explained, was one of the "charter congressmen" who introduced the equal-rights amendment in 1948 and has remained a "friend" of the movement. But she voted for Senator McGovern "because in this campaign he took the stronger position on E.R.A."

Today, at eighty-nine, Miss Paul no longer commutes regularly from her hillside home near Ridgefield, Connecticut, to the Washington headquarters of the National Woman's Party, which she founded in 1916. But her interest and influence in the crusade for women's rights remain undiminished. "I think that American women are further along than any other women in the world," she said. "But you can't have peace in a world in which some women or some men or some nations are at different stages of development. There is so much work to be done."

H * * * * *

ow did you first become interested in woman suffrage?

It wasn't something I had to think about. When the Quakers were founded in England in the 1600's, one of their principles was and is equality of the sexes. So I never had any other idea. And long before my time the Yearly Meeting in Philadelphia, which I still belong to, formed a committee to work for votes for women. The principle was always there.

Then you had your family's encouragement in your work?

My father—he was president of the Burlington County

[New Jersey] Trust Company—died when I was quite young, but he and Mother were both active in the Quaker movement. Mother was the clerk of the Friend's Meeting in our hometown. I would say that my parents supported all the ideals that I had.

In 1912 wasn't it a bit unusual for a woman to receive a Ph.D. degree?

Oh, no. There were no women admitted, of course, to the undergraduate school at the University of Pennsylvania, but there were a number of women graduate students.

When did you actually become involved in suffrage work?

Well, after I got my master's in 1907, my doctoral studies took me to the School of Economics in London. The English women were struggling hard to get the vote, and everyone was urged to come in and help. So I did. That's all there was to it. It was the same with Lucy Burns.

You met Miss Burns in London?

Yes, we met in a police station after we were both arrested. I had been asked to go on a little deputation that was being led by Mrs. [Emmeline] Pankhurst to interview the Prime Minister. I said I'd be delighted to go, but I had no idea that we'd be arrested. I don't know what the charge was. I suppose they hadn't made all the preparations for the interview with the Prime Minister or something. At any rate, I noticed that Miss Burns had a little American flag pin on her coat, so I went up to her, and we became great friends and allies and comrades. Well, we got out of that, and, of course, afterwards we were immediately asked to do something else. And that way you sort of get into the ranks.

Wh*at sort of things were you asked to do?*

The next thing I was asked to do was to go up to Norwich and "rouse the town," as they say. Winston Churchill was in the British cabinet and was going to make a speech there. Well, the English suffragists knew that the government was completely opposed to suffrage, and they conceived this plan to publicly ask all the cabinet members what they were going to do about votes for women. For that moment at least, the whole audience would turn to the subject of suffrage. We considered it an inexpensive way of advertising our cause. I thought it was a very successful method.

What happened at Norwich?

I went to Norwich with one other young woman, who was as inexperienced as I was, and we had street meetings in the marketplace, where everyone assembled for several nights before Mr. Churchill's speech. I don't know whether we exactly "roused the town," but by the time he arrived, I think Norwich was pretty well aware of what we were trying to do. The night he spoke, we had another meeting outside the hall. We were immediately arrested. You didn't have to be a good speaker, because the minute you began, you were arrested.

Were you a good speaker?

Not particularly. Some people enjoyed getting up in public like that, but I didn't. I did it, though. On the other hand, Lucy Burns was a very good speaker—she had what you call that gift of the Irish—and she was extremely courageous, a thousand times more courageous than I was. I was the timid type, and she was just naturally valiant. Lucy became one of the pillars of our movement. We never, never, never could have had such a campaign in this country without her.

In her book about the suffrage movement Inez Haynes Irwin tells about your hiding overnight on the roof of St. Andrew's Hall in Glasgow, Scotland, in order to break up a political rally the next day.

Did Mrs. Irwin say that? Oh, no. I never hid on any roof in my life. In Glasgow I was arrested, but it was at a street meeting we organized there. Maybe Mrs. Irwin was referring to the Lord Mayor's banquet in London. I think it was in December of 1909, and Miss Burns and I were asked to interrupt the Lord Mayor. I went into the hall, not the night before but early in the morning when the charwomen went to work, and I waited up in the gallery all day. That night Lucy went in down below with the banquet guests. I don't remember whether she got up and interrupted the mayor. I only remember that I did.

What happened?

I was arrested, of course.

Was this the time you were imprisoned for thirty days and forcibly fed to break your hunger strike?

I can't remember how long I was in jail that time. I was arrested a number of times. As for forcible feeding, I'm certainly not going to describe that.

The whole concept of forcible feeding sounds shocking.

Well, to me it was shocking that a government of men could look with such extreme contempt on a movement that was asking nothing except such a simple little thing as the right to vote. Seems almost unthinkable now, doesn't it? With all these millions and millions of women going out happily to work today, and nobody, as far as I can see, thinking there's anything unusual about it. But, of course, in some countries woman suffrage is still something that has to be won.

Do you credit Mrs. Pankhurst with having trained you in the militant tactics you subsequently introduced into the American campaign?

That wasn't the way the movement was, you know. Nobody was being trained. We were just going in and doing the simplest little things that we were asked to do. You see, the movement was very small in England, and small in this country, and small everywhere, I suppose. So I got to know Mrs. Pankhurst and her daughter, Christabel, quite well. I had, of course, a great veneration and admiration for Mrs. Pankhurst, but I wouldn't say that I was very much trained by her. What happened was that when Lucy Burns and I came back, having both been imprisoned in England, we were invited to take part in the campaign over here; otherwise nobody would have ever paid any attention to us.

That was in 1913?

I came back in 1910. It was in 1912 that I was appointed by the National American Woman Suffrage Association to the chairmanship of their Congressional Committee in Washington, which was to work for the passage of the amendment that Susan B. Anthony had helped draw up. And Lucy Burns was asked to go with me. Miss Jane Addams, who was on the national board, made the motion for our appointments. They didn't take the work at all seriously, or else they wouldn't have entrusted it to us, two young girls. They did make one condition, and that was that we should never send them any bills, for as much as one dollar. Everything we did, we must raise the money ourselves. My predecessor, Mrs. William Kent, the wife of the congressman from California, told me that she had been given ten dollars the previous year by the national association, and at the end of her term she gave back some change.

Weren't you discouraged by the national association's attitude?

Well, when we came along, we tried to do the work on a scale which we thought, in our great ignorance, might bring some success. I had an idea that it might be a one year's campaign. We would explain it to every congressman, and the amendment would go through. It was so clear. But it took us seven years. When you're young, when you've never done anything very much on your own, you imagine that it won't be so hard. We probably wouldn't

have undertaken it if we had known the difficulties.

How did you begin?

I went down to Washington on the seventh of December, 1912. All I had at the start was a list of people who had supported the movement, but when I tried to see them, I found that almost all of them had died or moved, and nobody knew much about them. So we were left with a tiny handful of people.

With all these obstacles how did you manage to organize the tremendous parade that greeted President-elect Wilson three months later?

Well, it wasn't such a tremendous parade. We called it a procession. I don't know whether there were five thousand or ten thousand marchers, maybe, but it wasn't a very big one. The idea for such a parade had been discussed at the 1912 suffrage convention, although some of the delegates thought it was too big an undertaking. It was unusual. There had never been a procession of women for any cause under the sun, so people did want to go and see it.

The press estimated the crowd at a half million. Whose idea was it to have the parade the day before Wilson's inaugural?

That was the only day you could have it if you were trying to impress the new President. The marchers came from all over the country at their own expense. We just sent letters everywhere, to every name we could find. And then we had a hospitality committee headed by Mrs. Harvey Wiley, the wife of the man who put through the first pure-food law in America. Mrs. Wiley canvassed all her friends in Washington and came up with a tremendous list of people who were willing to entertain the visiting marchers for a day or two. I mention these names to show what a wonderful group of people we had on our little committee.

Did you have any trouble getting a police permit?

No, although in the beginning the police tried to get us to march on Sixteenth Street, past the embassies and all. But from our point of view Pennsylvania Avenue was the place. So Mrs. Ebenezer Hill, whose husband was a Connecticut congressman and whose daughter Elsie was on our committee, she went to see the police chief, and we got our permit. We marched from the Capitol to the White House, and then on to Constitution Hall, which was the hall of the Daughters of the American Revolution, which many of our people were members of.

Didn't the parade start a riot?

The press reports said that the crowd was very hostile, but

it wasn't hostile at all. The spectators were practically all tourists who had come for Wilson's inauguration. We knew there would be a large turnout for our procession, because the company that put up the grandstands was selling tickets and giving us a small percentage. The money we got—it was a gift from heaven—helped us pay for the procession. I suppose the police thought we were only going to have a couple of hundred people, so they made no preparations. We were worried about this, so another member of our committee, Mrs. John Rogers, went the night before to see her brother-in-law, Secretary of War [Henry L.] Stimson, and he promised to send over the cavalry from Fort Myer if there was any trouble.

Did you need his help?

Yes, but not because the crowd was hostile. There were just so many people that they poured into the street, and we were not able to walk very far. So we called Secretary Stimson, and he sent over the troops, and they cleared the way for us. I think it took us six hours to go from the Capitol to Constitution Hall. Of course, we did hear a lot of shouted insults, which we always expected. You know, the usual things about why aren't you home in the kitchen where you belong. But it wasn't anything violent. Later on, when we were actually picketing the White House, the people did become almost violent. They would tear our banners out of our hands and that sort of thing.

Were you in the front ranks of the 1913 parade?

No. The national board members were at the head of it. I walked in the college section. We all felt very proud of ourselves, walking along in our caps and gowns. One of the largest and loveliest sections was made up of uniformed nurses. It was very impressive. Then we had a foreign section, and a men's section, and a Negro women's section from the National Association of Colored Women, led by Mary Church Terrell. She was the first colored woman to graduate from Oberlin, and her husband was a judge in Washington. Well, Mrs. Terrell got together a wonderful group to march, and then, suddenly, our members from the South said they wouldn't march. Oh, the newspapers just thought this was a wonderful story and developed it to the utmost. I remember that that was when the men's section came to the rescue. The leader, a Quaker I knew, suggested that the men march between the southern delegations and the colored women's section, and that finally satisfied the southern women. That was the greatest hurdle we had.

If the parade didn't cause any real trouble, why was there a subsequent congressional investigation that resulted in the ouster of the district police chief?

The principal investigation was launched at the request of our women delegates from Washington, which was a suffrage state. These women were so indignant about the remarks from the crowd. And I remember that Congressman Kent was very aroused at the things that were shouted at his daughter, Elizabeth, who was riding on the California float, and he was among the first in Congress to demand an investigation into why the police hadn't been better prepared. As I said, the police just didn't take our little procession seriously. I don't think it was anything intentional. We didn't testify against the police, because we felt it was just a miscalculation on their part.

What was your next move after the parade?

A few weeks after Mr. Wilson became President, four of us went to see him. And the President, of course, was polite and as much of a gentleman as he always was. He told of his own support, when he had been governor of New Jersey, of a state referendum on suffrage, which had failed. He said that he thought this was the way suffrage should come, through state referendums, not through Congress. That's all we accomplished. We said we were going to try and get it through Congress, that we would like to have his help and needed his support very much. And then we sent him another delegation and another and another and another and another and another and another—every type of women's group we could get. We did this until 1917, when the war started and the President said he couldn't see any more delegations.

So you began picketing the White House?

We said we would have a perpetual delegation right in front of the White House, so he wouldn't forget. Then they called it picketing. We didn't know enough to know what picketing was, I guess.

How did you finance all this work?

Well, as I mentioned, we were instructed not to submit any bills to the National American. Anything we did, we had to raise the money for it ourselves. So to avoid any conflict with them we decided to form a group that would work exclusively on the Susan B. Anthony amendment. We called it the Congressional Union for Woman's Suffrage. You see, the Congressional Committee was a tiny group, so the Congressional Union was set up to help with the lobbying, to help with the speechmaking, and especially to help in raising money. The first year we raised $27,000. It just came from anybody who wanted to help. Mostly small contributions. John McLean, the owner of the Washington *Post*, I think, gave us a thousand dollars. That was the first big gift we ever got.

The records indicate that you raised more than $750,000 over the first eight years. Did your amazing fund-raising efforts cause you any difficulties with the National American?

I know that at the end of our first year, at the annual convention of the National American, the treasurer got up—and I suppose this would be the same with any society in the world—she got up and made a speech, saying, "Well, this group of women has raised a tremendous sum of money, and none of it has come to my treasury," and she was very displeased with this. Then I remember that Jane Addams stood up and reminded the convention that we had been instructed to pay our own debts, and so that was all there was to it. Incidentally, the Congressional Union paid *all* the bills of that national convention, which was held in Washington that year. I remember we paid a thousand dollars for the rent of the hall. If you spend a hard time raising the money, you remember about it.

Were you upset about not being reappointed chairman of the Congressional Committee?

No, because they asked me to continue. But they said if I were the committee chairman, I would have to drop the Congressional Union. I couldn't be chairman of both. Some of the members on the National American board felt that all the work being put into the federal amendment wasn't a good thing for the entire suffrage campaign. I told them I had formed this Congressional Union and that I wanted to keep on with it.

Was it true, as some historians of the movement maintain, that the National American's president, Dr. Anna Shaw, was "suspicious" of unusual activity in the ranks?

No, I don't think she was. She came down to Washington frequently and spoke at our meetings, and she walked at the head of our 1913 procession. But I think we did make the mistake perhaps of spending too much time and energy just on the campaign. We didn't take enough time, probably, to go and explain to all the leaders why we thought [the federal amendment] was something that could be accomplished. You see, the National American took the position—not Miss Anthony, but the later people—that suffrage was something that didn't exist anywhere in the world, and therefore we would have to go more slowly and have endless state referendums to indoctrinate the men of the country.

Obviously you didn't agree with this. Was this what caused the Congressional Union to break with the National American?

We didn't break with the National American. In a sense

we were expelled. At the 1913 convention they made lots and lots of changes in the association's constitution. I don't recall what they were, and I didn't concern myself with the changes at the time. At any rate, the Congressional Union was affiliated with the National American under one classification, and they wrote to us and said if we would resign from that classification and apply for another classification, there would be a reduction in our dues. So we did what they told us, and then when we applied for the new classification, they refused to accept us, and we were out.

Why did the National American do this to your group?

The real division was over the Shafroth-Palmer amendment that the National American decided to substitute for the Anthony amendment in the spring of 1914. Under this proposal each state would hold a referendum on woman suffrage *if* more than 8 per cent of the legal voters in the last preceding election—males, of course—signed a petition for it. This tactic had been tried without much success before, and with all the time and money such campaigns involve, I don't think many women would have ever become voters. Our little group wanted to continue with the original amendment, which we called the Susan B. Anthony because the women of the country, if they knew anything about the movement, had heard the name Susan B. Anthony. Now the great part of the American women were very loyal to this amendment, and when the National American suddenly switched to Shafroth-Palmer, we thought that the whole movement was going off on a sidetrack. And that is the reason we later formed the National Woman's Party, because if we hadn't continued, there would have been nobody in Washington speaking up for the original amendment.

Y*ou didn't have much faith in state referendums?*

The first thing I ever did—after I graduated from Swarthmore, I did some social work in New York City—one of the suffragists there asked me to go with her to get signatures for a suffrage referendum in New York State. So I went with her, and she was a great deal older and much more experienced than I was. I remember going into a little tenement room with her, and a man there spoke almost no English, but he could vote. Well, we went in and tried to talk to this man and ask him to vote for equality for women. And almost invariably these men said, "No, we don't think that it is the right thing. We don't do that in Italy, women don't vote in Italy." You can hardly go through one of those referendum campaigns and not think what a waste of the strength of women to try and convert a majority of men in the state. From that day on I was convinced that the way to do it was through Congress, where there was a smaller group of people to work with.

Then the National Woman's Party was formed to continue the work on the federal amendment?

We changed our name from the Congressional Union to the National Woman's Party in 1916, when we began to get so many new members and branches. Mainly people who disagreed with the National American's support of the Shafroth-Palmer. And the person who got us to change our name was Mrs. [Alva E.] Belmont.

Would you tell me about Mrs. Belmont?

She was, of course, a great supporter of the suffrage movement financially, and we didn't even know her the first year we were in Washington. People said to me that she was a wonderfully equipped person who was very fond of publicity, and they suggested that I invite her to come down and sit on one of the parade floats. Well, I didn't know who she was at all, but I wrote her an invitation, and I remember thinking what a queer person she must be to want to sit on a float. She turned out to be anything but the type she was described, and, of course, she didn't sit on any float. Anyway, a year later, after we had been expelled from the National American and couldn't have been more alone and more unpopular and more unimportant, one of our members, Crystal Eastman [Benedict], contacted Mrs. Belmont. And Mrs. Belmont invited me to come have dinner and spend the night at her home in New York City. Well, I like to go to bed early, but Mrs. Belmont was the type that liked to talk all night. So all night we talked about how we could probably get suffrage. A little later Mrs. Belmont withdrew entirely from the old National American and threw her whole strength into our movement. The first thing she did was give us five thousand dollars. We had never had such a gift before.

Why do you think Mrs. Belmont crossed over to your group?

She was entirely in favor of our approach to the problem. She wanted to be immediately put on our national board, so she could have some direction. And then, after suffrage was won, she became the president of the Woman's Party, and at that time she gave us most of the money to buy the house in Washington that is still the party's headquarters. Over the years Mrs. Belmont did an enormous amount for the cause of women's equality. She was just one of those people who were born with the feeling of independence for herself and for women.

Did Mrs. Belmont have something to do with the decision to campaign against the Democrats in the November, 1914, elections?

Yes. You see, here we had an extremely powerful and won-derful man—I thought Woodrow Wilson was a very wonderful man—the leader of his party, in complete control of Congress. But when the Democrats in Congress caucused, they voted against suffrage. You just naturally felt that the Democratic Party was responsible. Of course, in England they were up against the same thing. They couldn't get this measure through Parliament without getting the support of the party that was in complete control.

Didn't this new policy of holding the party in power responsible represent a drastic change in the strategy of the suffrage movement?

Up to this point the suffrage movement in the United States had regarded each congressman, each senator, as a friend or a foe. It hadn't linked them together. And maybe these men were individual friends or foes in the past. But we deliberately asked the Democrats to bring it up in their caucus, and they did caucus against us. So you couldn't regard them as your allies anymore. I reported all this to the National American convention in 1913, and I said that it seemed to us that we must begin to hold this party responsible. And nobody objected to my report. But when we began to put it into operation, there was tremendous opposition, because people said that this or that man has been our great friend, and here you are campaigning against him.

Would you have taken the same position against the Republicans if that party had been in power in 1914?

Of course. You see, we tried very hard in 1916—wasn't it [Charles Evans] Hughes running against Wilson that year? —to get the Republicans to put federal suffrage in their platform, and we failed. We also failed with the Democrats. Then we tried to get the support of Mr. Hughes himself. Our New York State committee worked very hard on Mr. Hughes, and they couldn't budge him. So we went to see former President [Theodore] Roosevelt at his home at Oyster Bay to see if *he* could influence Mr. Hughes. And I remember so vividly what Mr. Roosevelt said. He said, "You know, in political life you must always remember that you not only must be on the right side of a measure, but you must be on the right side at the right time." He told us that that was the great trouble with Mr. Hughes, that Mr. Hughes is certainly for suffrage, but he can't seem to know that he must do it in time. So Mr. Hughes started on his campaign around the country, and when he came to Wyoming, where women were already voting, he wouldn't say he was for the suffrage amendment. And he went on and on, all around the country. Finally, when he came to make his final speech of the campaign in New York, he had made up his mind, and he came out strongly for the federal suffrage amendment. So it was true what Mr. Roosevelt had said about him.

Do you think Hughes might have beaten Wilson in 1916 if he had come out for suffrage at the beginning of his campaign?

Oh, I don't know about that. I was just trying to show you that we were always trying to get the support of both parties.

Well, this decision to politically attack the party in power, could this be attributed to the influence of Mrs. Pankhurst and your experience in England?

Maybe, although I didn't ever really think about it as being that. The key was really the two million women who were already enfranchised voters in the eight western suffrage states. One fifth of the Senate, one seventh of the House, and one sixth of the electoral votes came from the suffrage states, and it was really a question of making the two political parties aware of the political power of women. This was also part of my report to the 1913 National American convention. I said that this was a weapon we could use—taking away votes in the suffrage states from the party in power—to bring both parties around to the federal amendment more quickly.

In the 1914 elections women voted for forty-five members of Congress, and the Democrats won only nineteen of these races, often by drastically reduced pluralities. Weren't you at all concerned about defeating some of your strongest Democratic supporters in Congress?

Not really. Whoever was elected from a suffrage state was going to be prosuffrage in Congress anyway, whether he was Republican or Democrat. But how else were we going to demonstrate that women could be influential, independent voters? One of the men we campaigned against was Representative—later Senator—Carl Hayden of Arizona, and he finally became a very good friend of the movement, I thought. But it is true that most of them really did resent it very much.

You mean like Representative Taggart of Kansas?

Who? I don't remember him.

Taggart was the man who attacked you personally at the Judiciary Committee hearings on December 16, 1914. His election majority had been cut from 3,000 in 1912 to 300 in 1914, and when you appeared before the committee to testify on the federal amendment, he said, "Are you here to report the progress of your efforts to defeat Democratic candidates?" He was very upset.

Evidently. But I really don't remember that, although I know that that feeling was fairly general among the men we had campaigned against. You see, we had so many, many of these hearings. I don't try to remember them. I sort of wiped them all out of my mind because all of that is past.

I mentioned this particular hearing because the man who came to your defense that day was Representative Volstead, the author of Prohibition, which had a great impact on woman suffrage by removing one of your most vigorous enemies, the liquor lobby.

Oh? I wouldn't know what you call the liquor lobby, but certainly the liquor interests in the country were represented at the hearings against us. They had some nice dignified name, but they were always there, and I suppose they are still in opposition to our equal-rights amendment. People have the idea that women are the more temperate half of the world, and I hope they are, although I don't know for sure. The prohibitionists supported our efforts, but I didn't have any contact with them. And I wasn't a member of the Women's Christian Temperance Union at that time. I've since become a member.

B*y the way, what was the significance of the movement's official colors?*

The purple, white, and gold? I remember the person who chose those colors for us, Mrs. John J. White. She noticed that we didn't have a banner at the 1913 procession, so she said, "I am going to have a banner made for you, a beautiful banner that will be identified with the women's movement." So she had a banner made with these colors, and we agreed to it. There wasn't any special significance to the choice of colors. They were just beautiful. It may be an instinct, it is with me anyway, when you're presenting something to the world, to make it as beautiful as you can.

You were once quoted to the effect that in picking volunteers you preferred enthusiasm to experience.

Yes. Well, wouldn't you? I think everybody would. I think every reform movement needs people who are full of enthusiasm. It's the first thing you need. I was full of enthusiasm, and I didn't want any lukewarm person around. I still am, of course.

One of your most enthusiastic volunteers was Inez Milholland Boissevain, wasn't she?

Inez Milholland actually gave her life for the women's movement. I think Inez was our most beautiful member. We always had her on horseback at the head of our processions. You've probably read about this, but when Inez was a student at Vassar, she tried to get up a suffrage meeting, and the college president refused to let her hold the meeting. So she organized a little group, and they jumped over a wall at the edge of the college and held the first suffrage meeting at Vassar in a cemetery. Imagine such a thing happening at a women's college so short a time ago. You can hardly believe such things occurred. But they did.

How did Miss Milholland give her life for the movement?

After college Inez wanted to study law, but every prominent law school refused to admit a girl. She finally went to New York University, which wasn't considered much of a university then, and got her law degree. Then she threw her whole soul into the suffrage movement and really did nothing else but that. Well, in 1916, when we were trying to prevent the re-election of Woodrow Wilson, we sent speakers to all the suffrage states, asking people not to vote for Wilson, because he was opposing the suffrage which they already had. Inez and her sister, Vita, who was a beautiful singer, toured the suffrage states as a team. Vita would sing songs about the women's movement, and then Inez would speak. Their father, John Milholland, paid all the expenses for their tour, which began in Wyoming. Well, when they got to Los Angeles, Inez had just started to make her speech when she suddenly collapsed and fell to the floor, just from complete exhaustion. Her last words were "Mr. President, how long must women wait for liberty?" We used her words on picket banners outside the White House. I think she was about twenty-eight or twenty-nine.

What happened then?

She was brought back and buried near her family home in New York State. We decided to have a memorial service for her in Statuary Hall in the Capitol on Christmas Day. So I asked Maud Younger, who was our congressional chairman and a great speaker, if she would make the principal speech at the ceremony. Maud said she had never made this kind of speech before and asked me how to do it. I remember telling her, "You just go and read Lincoln's Gettysburg Address and then you will know just how." Maud made a wonderful speech, as she always did.

Did you have any difficulties getting permission to hold the Milholland service in Statuary Hall?

When you have a small movement without much support, you sometimes run into difficulties. I don't remember any particular difficulty, but we always had them. You just take things in your stride, don't you think? If you come up against all these obstacles, well, you've got to do something about them if you want to get through to the end you have in view. In this case we wanted to show our gratitude to Inez Milholland, and we wanted the world to realize—and I think they did—the importance of her contribution by holding it in the Capitol and having so many people of

national importance attend.

Did you invite President Wilson and his family?

Oh, no. We did send a delegation to him from the meeting, but he wouldn't receive them. Finally on January 9, 1917, he agreed to meet with women from all over the country who brought Milholland resolutions. The women asked him once more to lend the weight and influence of his great office to the federal amendment, but the President rejected the appeal and continued to insist that he was the follower, not the leader, of his party. The women were quite disappointed when they returned to Cameron House, where we had established our headquarters across Lafayette Square from the White House. That afternoon we made the decision to have a perpetual delegation, six days a week, from ten in the morning until half past five in the evening, around the White House. We began the next day.

And this perpetual delegation, or picketing, continued until the President changed his position?

Yes. Since the President had made it clear that he wouldn't see any more delegations in his office, we felt that pickets outside the White House would be the best way to remind him of our cause. Every day when he went out for his daily ride, as he drove through our picket line he always took off his hat and bowed to us. We respected him very much. I always thought he was a great President. Years later, when I was in Geneva [Switzerland] working with the World Woman's Party, I was always so moved when I would walk down to the League of Nations and see the little tribute to Woodrow Wilson.

Do you think that the President's daughters, Jessie and Margaret, who were strong supporters of the suffrage movement, exerted any pressure on the President?

Well, I think if you live in a home and have two able daughters—the third daughter was younger, and I didn't know much about what she was doing—it would almost be inevitable that the father would be influenced. Also, I think the first Mrs. Wilson was very sympathetic to us, but we never knew Mrs. Galt, his second wife. Someone told me that she wrote a book recently about her life in the White House in which she spoke in the most derogatory terms about the suffragists.

Do you want to talk about the violence that occurred on the White House picket line?

Not particularly. It is true that after the United States entered the war [April 6, 1917], there was some hostility, and some of the pickets were attacked and had their banners ripped out of their hands. The feeling was—and some of

CONTINUED ON PAGE 92

On any list of events that have altered the course of history the opening of Japan to foreign trade in 1854 must surely rank high. While the United States was pushing its boundaries westward to the Pacific and reaching the early stages of industrialization, Japan lay cradled in the tight shell of its own seventeenth century. Under an absolute ban on intercourse with the rest of the world imposed in 1638, Japanese citizens could not leave the islands, and foreigners could not enter them. No seagoing vessels were built, and Japanese fishermen shipwrecked on foreign shores were not allowed to return. The only contact permitted with the outside world was a very limited trade with certain Chinese, Korean, and Dutch merchants.

For the United States, Japan's impervious isolation was a problem and a challenge. Steam vessels could be used in the China trade only if coaling stations could be found; American whalers who wandered into Japanese coastal waters needed protection and provisioning. Establishing relations with Japan was becoming imperative by 1850.

The deed might have been done by force; the British had won concessions from China during the previous decade by waging the Opium War. The United States assigned to the task Commodore Matthew C. Perry, who chose instead to use all of the arts of diplomacy to win Japanese friendship and respect as well as a trade agreement.

Few American diplomatic missions have employed so many different kinds of art in diplomacy as the Perry expedition to Japan used in 1854. Like other emissaries before and since, Perry alternately threatened and cajoled, exercising the skill that is usually referred to in the phrase "art of diplomacy." But Perry went further: from initial contact to final treaty he made extensive use of the physical arts and crafts of his country to help persuade the secluded island empire to open its

A TYPICAL AMERICAN TREATY BINDING AND SKIPPET OF THE
MID-NINETEENTH CENTURY, FROM THE NATIONAL ARCHIVES

As well as the art of diplomacy, there are also the Arts of diplomacy

By
VIRGINIA CARDWELL PURDY

25

ports to Western trade, ending two centuries of isolation.

In careful preparation for the mission, gifts were chosen to please the rulers of Japan and to impress them with the wealth of the United States and the superiority of its fine and practical arts. Since the recently issued final volume of John J. Audubon's *The Viviparous Quadrupeds of North America* was much coveted at a thousand dollars a copy, the five volumes of this work and its companion, *The Birds of America*, appeared to be presents fit for an emperor. Live plant and tree specimens were carefully tended during the voyage by the "agriculturist" of the expedition: forty oak trees, half red and half white; many fruit and ornamental trees; one poinsettia; and one prickly pear. Wine and whiskey, perfume and mirrors were packed in with pumps and plows, stoves and weapons. To demonstrate the novel art of photography a daguerreotype camera was included to take presentation portraits of Japanese officials. A working telegraph was expected to show the Japanese the latest thing in communications.

The most remarkable gift, however, was a quarter-size model railroad, perfect in every detail down to a quarter-size coal bucket, made by the Norris Locomotive Works of Philadelphia. The steel, brass, and copper steam locomotive, tender, and coach reached a speed of 15.7 miles an hour on a circular track 370.5 feet long with a passenger or two astride the handsome rosewood passenger carriage made by the Kinball and Gorton Company. For all of this the Department of State paid $4,065.

As a result of Perry's efforts articles of agreement were completed, and drafts were prepared in Japanese and English to be signed by the plenipotentiaries of both nations. Perry's copy, the American "original" copy of the treaty, was brought back to the United States for President Pierce to send to the Senate for its advice and consent. In appearance it was a very simple document.

As a final impressive flourish, however, a good deal of money and effort were invested in the preparation of the American "exchange copy," which was signed by the President and returned to Japan to signify the ratification of the agreement by Perry's government. A large wax impression of the Great Seal of the United States was attached to the document with golden cords and encased in a gold box, or skippet. Samuel Lewis, a Washington jeweler, was paid $1,220.52 for the skippet and for gold hinges, buttons,

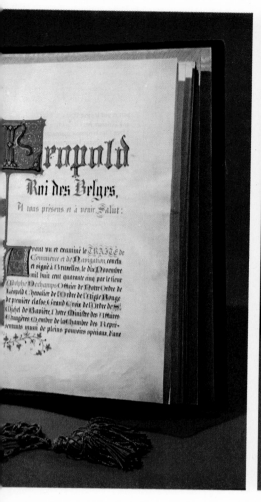

screws, and a lock for the velvet-lined rosewood box in which treaty and skippet were placed.

In sending out an important diplomatic mission laden with rare and expensive gifts and in commissioning a handsome and costly binding, skippet, and treaty box for the Perry treaty, the United States government was actually conforming to European diplomatic custom—a conformity the United States had at first resisted as incompatible with a republican system. In Europe by the end of the eighteenth century the exchange copy of a treaty was often an elaborate work of art designed to reflect the majesty and culture of the royal personage whose signature appeared on the final page. And ostentatious gift-giving among monarchs and diplomats presented further opportunities to pay subtle compliments to foreign potentates while boasting silently of the wealth and skills of the donor's country.

Into this world of opulent diplomacy the United States had stepped in 1776 with utopian principles and empty hands. The principles were quite sincere. Steeped in the idealism of the eighteenth-century *philosophes*, many Americans felt messianic stirrings. They believed that their new nation would lead the decadent Old World into a

At left, the Louisiana Purchase treaty of 1803 reflects France's new republican spirit. The initials P.F. *on the purple velvet binding stand for* Peuple Français, *and on the gold-washed silver skippet a symbolic female figure and the legend* Au Nom du Peuple Français *proclaim* la République. *In the center is a commercial treaty with Belgium signed in 1845. Its velvet binding is undecorated, but the elegant document inside looks like a medieval illuminated manuscript. Belgium's royal arms adorn the silver skippet. The gorgeous object at right is a 1908 Chinese letter of credence to introduce a new imperial minister to President Theodore Roosevelt. The richly embroidered cover is of yellow silk.*
ALL: NATIONAL ARCHIVES

period of international relations based on "right, not might" and characterized by open dealings under international law. By eliminating power politics Thomas Jefferson expected American policy to achieve "the total emancipation of commerce and the bringing together all nations for a free intercommunication of happiness." Nothing that smacked of corruption must be permitted.

Of course, the poverty of the new American government was also grimly genuine. But the idealism permitted the country's first diplomats to make a virtue of its indigence.

27

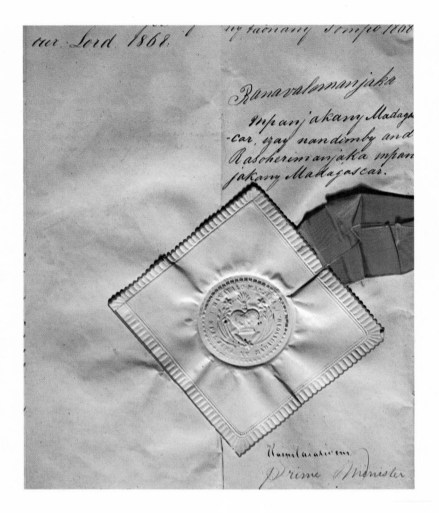

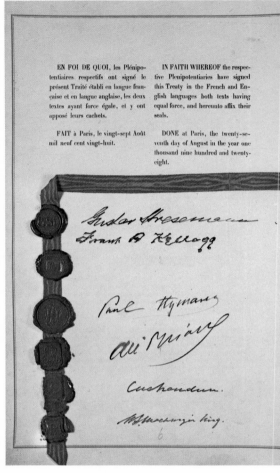

With fine contempt they considered the glittering courts with their ceremonious forms and ornate ostentation to be symbols of the frivolous cynicism of traditional diplomacy. Sent by the Continental Congress to plead the American cause in France early in 1776, Silas Deane wrote piously to the Secret Committee of Congress, "Parade and Pomp have no charms in the eyes of a patriot, or even of a man of common good sense." Benjamin Franklin made his fur cap an emblem of republican simplicity, and Abigail Adams described the gown she wore when she was presented at the Court of St. James's in 1784 as "elegant, but plain as I could possibly appear, with decency."

It might have been expected that this persistent nonconformity would carry over into other ceremonial and decorative aspects of American foreign relations. But American representatives abroad soon began to discover that there was more than mere gratification of vanity in the extravagant etiquette and elegant style of diplomatic exchanges. They learned that they must take subtleties of rank and deference into consideration if they were to serve their own country effectively. As John Adams gloomily observed, "We must submit to what we cannot alter."

Soon the Continental Congress itself began to seek for the United States all the accouterments of nationhood. The members devoted much thought to the creation of a Great Seal, finally settling on a strong and simple design that has remained essentially unchanged ever since. It is described in the journal of the Continental Congress for June 20, 1782, in very unrepublican heraldic terms: "Paleways of thirteen pieces, argent and gules . . ."

In treaty bindings, however, the United States at first exhibited an austerity of taste commensurate with its Puritan ideals. The Treaty of Paris of 1783 was a paper book without a cover, held together by the seal ribbons. The Jay Treaty of 1795 was also sent to Great Britain with no cover. The seal was applied through paper on red wax over blue ribbons on the signature page.

But it was not long before the Department of State had fallen completely in line with European custom in this regard. On March 13, 1815, one Joseph Milligan was paid sixty dollars for a "Portfolio of green velvet, lined with orange silk, tied with red, white, blue and yellow Ribband. —Gold Cord and Tassels, with Silver Box and Seal appendant" for the exchange copy of the Treaty of Ghent at the

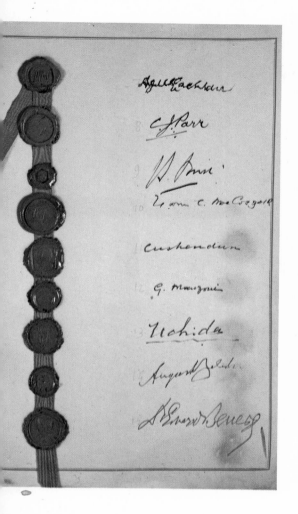

By the middle of the nineteenth century the skippet was going out of fashion, and seals wafered or pressed onto the signature page of a treaty became standard. At far left the royal seal of Queen Rana-valomanjaka of Madagascar is affixed over pink silk ribbon on this treaty of friendship with the United States in 1868. The Kellogg-Briand Pact to outlaw war, at center, was eventually signed by forty-seven more hopeful countries in 1928. Briand's signature is the fourth on the list. Lord Cushendun signed twice, once for Britain and once for India. The seals were pressed in wax over red ribbon. The lacy Bavarian naturalization treaty seal of 1868, above, looks like some charming international valentine from the days when diplomats acted on "All-Highest Royal Command."

end of the War of 1812.

In 1824 a larger, more imposing seal die was ordered by the Department of State for pendant seals. From about 1833 until 1852 F. Masi & Company, a "Military and Fancy store" in Washington, supplied the department with treaty accessories. By midcentury the Department of State had fallen so far from republican grace that the typical American instrument of ratification was bound in velvet and bore a silver skippet attached with silver cord and tassels. Treaty boxes were usually satin-lined morocco with ornamental gold stampings.

By the late 1860's some nations began to eliminate skippets. In February, 1871, Secretary of State Hamilton Fish asked his chief of the First Diplomatic Bureau, H. D. J. Pratt, to determine "what style of box & of seal do the Foreign Govt. use with the treaties they send here?" Pratt replied that the boxes varied in elegance from some made of "fancy woods," ornamental morocco, or velvet to "merely pasteboard pouches, covered [in buckram]. . . ." He further observed:

Nearly all the treaties are in velvet covers with metallic seal boxes, mostly silver, and are arranged like those prepared here, with bullion cords and tassels.

The French and some of the German States have not used metallic seals to recent treaties but have substituted paper seals affixed to the body of the ratifications. . . .

Fish scribbled across the top of the report, "Have no more fancy boxes made & no more metallic cases for seals." The last payment for skippets was made in 1870 to Samuel Lewis: $720 for "six silver treaty boxes." Probably the last one used was attached to the 1871 Treaty of Washington with Great Britain.

Although a few other nations continued to use pendant

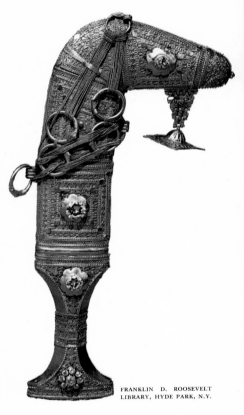

seals and skippets for some time, today most countries use simple gold-tooled morocco bindings and wafered paper seals. Sad to relate, some of the great recent multilateral agreements in the custody of the Department of State are now typewritten and bound in buckram.

If the Founding Fathers had difficulty reconciling themselves to monarchical customs requiring that treaties be accompanied by artistic trappings, the question of diplomatic gifts created an even stickier problem. The men who drafted the Constitution thought they were taking care of the matter in Article I, Section 9, which provides that

> no Person holding any Office of Profit or Trust under them [the United States], shall, without the consent of the Congress, accept of any present, Emolument, Office, or Title of any kind whatever, from any King, Prince, or foreign State.

There seems to have been very little real debate on the subject in the Constitutional Convention. James Madison's notes record only that, in support of Article I, Section 9,

"Mr. Pinckney urged the necessity of preserving foreign ministers, and other officers of the United States, independent of external influence." Edmund Randolph explained to the Virginia Ratification Convention that a particular incident had prompted the inclusion of this prohibition in the Constitution. Benjamin Franklin had accepted a gift, probably a snuff box with a portrait of Louis XVI on it, from the king of France. "It was thought proper," Randolph declared,

> in order to exclude corruption and foreign influence, to prohibit any one in office from receiving or holding any emoluments from foreign states. I believe, that if at that moment, when we were in harmony with the king of France, we had supposed that he was corrupting our ambassador, it might have disturbed that confidence, and diminished that mutual friendship, which contributed to carry us through the war.

Nothing in the Federalist Papers deals with receiving gifts. But in discussing the reasons for having the Senate "advise and consent" to the ratification of treaties, Alex-

ander Hamilton observed that the President might be "tempted to betray the interests of the State for the acquisition of wealth," considering the fact that a man might be

> raised from the station of a private citizen to the rank of chief magistrate, possessed of a moderate or slender fortune, and looking forward to a period not very remote when he may probably be obliged to return to the station from which he was taken.

Europeans apparently accepted without comment the austerity of Americans who joined the diplomatic corps in their capitals, but to the Moslem potentates of North Africa and the Near East a failure to exchange presents was an example of very bad manners, if not an expression of ill will. Recognizing this attitude, American policy alternated between a rather relaxed acceptance of established patterns within the spirit of the Constitution and occasional fierce attacks of conscience that caused strict adherence to its letter. In 1796, for example, Consul Joel Barlow reported that he had been welcomed by the dey of Algiers with a gift of "a fine Barbary stallion," and President

International gift-giving allows a nation to display its creative arts in furthering its diplomatic ends. At far left are two sculptures carved from elephant tusks and illuminated from within; they were presented to President Kennedy by Prime Minister Nehru in 1961. F.D.R. received the diamond-studded dagger at left in 1945 from King ibn Saud of Saudi Arabia. Only one inch wide and circled with diamonds, this tiny miniature of a Siamese king was presented to President Hoover in 1930. The ancient stone sculpture above dates from the first century B.C. and depicts episodes in the life of Buddha. In 1969 the president of Pakistan gave it to President Nixon. The roofs of the huts of the two-inch-high village above are removable to show the interiors. This is one of a set of polychrome cast-metal figures presented to President Johnson in 1965 by the President of the republic of Upper Volta in Africa.

Washington expressed pleasure that he had been received so graciously. But when, in 1795, Pierre Adet, the French minister to the United States, presented George Washington with the colors of France on behalf of the French Committee of Safety, Washington replied formally:

> I receive, sir . . . the colors of France, which you have

CONTINUED ON PAGE 89

THE *W*AY TO *A*LASKA

By WALTER HAVIGHURST

Among the visitors who tour Alaskan Way, the noisy street that arcs the Seattle waterfront, a few may wonder how to get to Alaska from there. Ships from Wrangell, Juneau, Sitka, and Skagway used to berth there, but their last passengers crossed the gangway in 1954. Until then Seattle harbor was the jumping-off place for the North, steamships heading up through the Inside Passage and schooners coming down with yellow deckloads of spruce and hemlock. Now the takeoff is from the Seattle-Tacoma airport, where jets roar up into the rain. They touch down at Juneau three hours later, with breakfast on the way. A half century ago it was a week's voyage to Alaska, and the lumber schooners took four times that long.

In 1923 downtown Seattle was beginning to spread northward and up the hill, and Pioneer Square with its tall totem pole in the little triangular park was not yet abandoned to skid row. Between voyages I lived down there in the three-story North Star Hotel, and I hung out in the Shipping Board's hiring hall near the Colman Dock on Alaskan Way, or Railroad Avenue, as it was then called. One assignment I wanted was a run to Alaska. There were two regular services to what the travel literature called the "Top o' the World," the Alaska Steamship Company and the Admiral Line. When ships docked at Pier 2,

next to the Colman Ferry, I watched men come ashore—loggers, fishermen, old sourdoughs, young cannery hands, a few Indians—and wondered about the little towns up there under the huge mountains. Having made the China run in an Admiral liner, I was hoping for a job on one of their Alaska ships. There were four of them: *Admiral Dewey, Admiral Rogers, Admiral Evans,* and *Admiral Watson.* These "modern, fast and commodious vessels" were pictured in the Admiral Line's window on Second Avenue. The *Dewey* was the newest and largest, but they all looked fine to me.

A recent reading of Ernest Gruening's account of "Alaska: The Last Frontier" led me to unearth some old notebooks, and I found a grubby item called Pheasant Pocket Notes. Beneath a faded picture of a ring-necked bird are lines for Name and School. My name is inked there, less dimmed than one would expect after fifty-one years, and my school also. The school is "Pacific Ocean." I think I remember buying the notebook in a secondhand bookstore on the corner of First Avenue and Yesler Way, but I had forgot about the pheasant and the school. At the top of the inside page is my word "Log." In 1923 I was compiling thoughts rather than actualities—a literary error common to the young— and the log makes queasy reading now. It begins with the spacious obser-

vation that the countries of the world are encircled by the unknown, just as the continents are but islands in the encompassing sea. Box the compass then, it exhorts me, to all the horizons of truth and understanding. These transcendental notes, I find, mostly ignore the daily encounters on the skid road and the harbor. But memory holds on to a few of them.

On one of my visits to the Admiral Line window, where I studied the big map of Alaska, I saw a towering man with long white hair under a Texas hat greeting everyone on Second Avenue like an indulgent king among his people. He spoke to me: "God bless you, young man," and a bit startled in my paint-stained dungarees, I said "Yes, sir." After he had passed, someone said, "That's Mark Matthews, the greatest preacher in America." On Sunday morning, in my shore clothes, I barely got into his church; he had a huge and hearty congregation. My log calls the sermon "dull and patronizing," but all I remember of the Reverend Mr. Matthews is his benign greeting on Second Avenue.

My blessing came promptly. "Monday morning, March 18," my log says, "shipped on lumber schooner for Alaska." I had learned to get to the hiring hall early on Monday mornings. When I came in the agent was writing on the blackboard "4 O.S. Schooner Snohomish towing S.E. Alaska for lumber." I was the first man to ask for the job, and while he wrote out my assignment to the schooner at the Connecticut Street pier, my mind filled with pictures of the rugged coastline and the storied towns at the Top o' the World.

I went to the North Star, stuffed my shore clothes along with Shelley and Dante into my seabag, and walked through a thin drizzle to the Connecticut Street basin. It would be a slow run, but I would really see the Inside Passage and have a good payday at the end. Ordinary seamen drew sixty-five dollars a month in 1923.

At the foot of Connecticut Street the *Snohomish* stood above the clutter of lumber and fishing docks. She was an old four-master, tired and dirty, her topmasts lifting into the fine rain. She still had her rigging but no canvas. Like other West Coast sailing vessels, she had become a barge. Instead of leaning white sails into the wind she would plod behind a grimy tugboat. But as I crossed the cleated gangplank she looked good to me.

The deck was littered and lifeless, but a wisp of smoke came from the galley. I looked in there. A morose, dark, dishevelled man was spooning coffee into a battered pot. "Keep out of the galley," he said sharply. I asked for the mate—a sailor reports to the mate with his assignment notice. He shook his head. "No mate here. Captain Olson's in his cabin." He opened the stove door and poked in a piece of slabwood. "Where's the fo'c's'le?" I asked. He pointed through a small square opening in the bulkhead—the slot through which would be thrust all the meals I would eat for weeks to come.

I went around the deckhouse, ducked under the door, and stepped down into the fo'c's'le. It was dark and clammy and smelled of damp straw mattresses. There were eight empty bunks and a bare mess table. I threw my bag into an upper bunk dimly lighted by a glassed porthole. Then I went aft to the cabin. A voice answered my knock, and I said, "Seaman reporting." The door opened and I handed my slip to a stocky, gray, unshaven man in a flecked gray undershirt with suspenders dangling from his trousers.

"Keep out of the cook's way," he said. "It's hard to keep a cook on this run."

My log, I find, says little about things that would interest me now, over a half century later. After observing that the schooner tugged at her lines like a mind tied to tenets in a classroom (in 1923 I was enjoying a grudge against college), it says "Worked by for two days, mostly cleaning out the hold, and in the Wednesday morning rain I steered out behind the Canadian tug *Coutli*." During those two days the other three seamen came aboard, and I would like to know what wary things we said to each other at that dim mess table and how my shipmates struck me at first sight. Instead of such reporting

Paint scraper in hand, Ordinary Seaman Havighurst poses with a shipmate in 1923.
AUTHOR'S COLLECTION

the log remarks: "Every vessel outward bound is a microcosm, a small, uneasy world seeking its own destiny."

Memory, however, has held on to the plain facts of that rainy Wednesday morning. Fuming and churning, the *Coutli* came alongside. She whistled, a big blast from a small craft, and Captain Olson came out of his cabin. The *Coutli* threw us a heaving line, and we hauled up a big hairy hawser and made fast. Probably because I was wearing my baggy Admiral Line sweater, the captain said to me, "You take the wheel, Slim." I immediately ran back to the pilothouse while the

tug whistled again.

On the raised deck astern the wheel was enclosed by a slant-roofed shed—except for a wide front window it looked exactly like a privy. As the towline stretched out, water rained from it onto the gray harbor. Then the *Snohomish* began to move, and I pulled on the old steering wheel. We crept by some anchored ships in Elliott Bay, past a big gray battlewagon heading in to Bremerton, and on up Puget Sound. My job was to follow the tugboat, and with that six-inch towline I couldn't have done anything else. Off Point No Point we were overtaken by the *Admiral Dewey*. As she swished past us, "modern, fast and commodious," two sailors at the bow beckoned me aboard. I waved them on. They would be in Juneau long before we were beyond Vancouver Island, but I wouldn't have traded places.

Years later I put a schooner and a tugboat into a story. I named the tug *Samson*, but she was just the *Coutli*, a battered little workhorse with her stern in white water and a smudge from her funnel. The *Coutli* carried four men, a cook, and a captain, just like us, and I soon knew them all by sight. On that small craft there was no place to go. When they came out of their messroom, they stood in the stern, staring at their tall-masted burden. We stared back. Day and night, for two thousand miles, we were just three hundred feet apart, and we never even waved to one another.

Captain Olson lived a solitary life in his cabin. The cook carried his meals aft on a tray, and every morning I filled his lamp with kerosene and trimmed the wick. He kept a neat cabin, with a pile of old *Capper's Farmer* magazines on the floor and some limp clothes on a line of sail twine. He always stood on deck after supper, feet apart in the chill wind and a pinch of snuff under his lip, scowling at the *Coutli*. Every time they threw coal on the fire, we had a rain of soot and cinders. I suppose he was thinking that with all that smoke they had warm quarters and could dry their clothes. Our main heat was in the galley, and the cook lived there; his bunk-room opened off the pantry. We had a donkey engine on deck, and we kept a fire

33

in the boiler. It gave us hot water and a place to warm our hands after a cold wheel-watch.

Two men to a watch, we spent four hours on and four off. The daytime watch meant two hours in the pilot shed and two hours poking around with a scraper and a paintbrush; at night it was two hours steering and two hours lookout—looking at the *Coutli*'s riding lights through the rain and once in a while at the glimmer of a Tlingit village under the mountains. The only instruments in our wheel house were a dry compass and a marine clock that chimed the half-hours—which the wheelsman answered with taps on the schooner's bell. The lookout station was on the bow, but we generally stood the watch

The schooner Snohomish *rests beside a wharf at Spruce Inlet, Alaska, waiting to be loaded with lumber. Her four masts are mere relics; a tug will tow her back to Seattle.*
AUTHOR'S COLLECTION

beside the donkey engine or in the pilot shanty with the wheelsman.

Captain Olson had been in the Lighthouse Service, he told me, and sometimes the *Snohomish* must have seemed as stationary as the Blind Channel Light. With a tide against us in the narrows the *Coutli* labored, the towline stretched out, and the mountains stopped moving. For four hours you could hear the same waterfall. At other times the tide swirled us through.

In the tiderips we came charging after the *Coutli*, our topmasts tossing and the towline under water.

In the wide waters of Dixon Entrance, where the long Pacific swell comes in, we met a liner, perhaps the *Admiral Dewey*, on her return voyage. She was ablaze with light. "Ships that pass in the night," my log says. "Does anyone there wonder what men and what thoughts are in this old schooner with a lantern flickering at her masthead?"

I find a few notes on my shipmates. The cook was morose and talkative; that is, he talked to himself. We would hear him through the galley bulkhead, his voice rising and falling in fervor and intimacy. We called him Frenchy; I don't know why. One night he let me

in the galley. He poured some coffee beside the stove and said that in Seattle he walked all night, all over the city, thinking. He thought about the world, how it was drowning in delusion and darkness and couldn't find the light. My log approves him as "a man against the world, as all men should be." He was already beat, back there in the careless 1920's.

The three other seamen were Rowley, Gibbs, and a Swede we called

Donkey—he claimed to understand the donkey engine. Rowley was just out of the army and wearing GI pants and wrap puttees along with a two-ply logger's shirt and a corduroy cap. He was dirty, lazy, boastful, and lying. My log notes that the captain called him "'a damn hoodlum'—which he is." That was the night when the captain found the wheel seesawing in the empty shanty and Rowley tending a coffeepot in the firebox of the donkey engine. Rowley wanted to go gold hunting in Siberia. He had heard of a bonanza there, and with that vague objective he was heading north. I agreed to go with him, for the sake of conversation in the night hours.

Gibbs was as solid and steady as the mast that grew like a spruce trunk through our fo'c's'le. He was older than the rest of us, thirty perhaps. One midnight when I relieved him at the wheel, he stood for a while in the shanty door. It was a clear, still night with a moon just past the full. Above the gleaming waters rose dark mountains, and the moon gleamed again on their icy summits. Half to me and half to the mystery around us Gibbs repeated, "They that go down to the sea in ships, that do business in great waters, they see God's wonders in the deep." I find pasted in my log a card he gave me:

A TIP
JOIN THE I.W.W.
Educational Meetings Every
Thursday Evening
Seattle Hall
512½ Second Ave.   Seattle, Wash.

The other side is more emphatic.

GET A KICK OUT OF LIFE
JOIN THE INDUSTRIAL WORKERS
OF THE WORLD

Gibbs was a surprising man. One night he startled me by quoting Shelley's "Masque of Anarchy," his steady voice keeping those rhythms above the creak of the steering gear.

Rise like Lions after slumber
In unvanquishable number,
Shake your chains to earth like dew
Which in sleep had fallen on you—
Ye are many—they are few.

I wanted to say something about Shelley, living at Villa Valsavano in the gnarled old olive groves of Tuscany, not knowing that his words would be repeated under the mountains of Alaska—a name he never knew. But Gibbs had begun talking about money, the myth of money, the printed paper that won't feed a man who is hungry, or warm a man who is cold. The things produced by human toil are real, he said, but money is a myth perpetuated by the few in order to control the many. Then he told me he had been a homesteader on the Peace River above Edmonton, until a forest fire burned him out. (I could see him winterbound in his cabin, sitting by the stove with his black hair freshly combed, reading a Bible and a book of poems while the snow piled up outside.) Since then he had worked in sawmills and on lumber wharves—up and down the coast from Vancouver to San Pedro. He had joined the Wobblies in Seattle, and he sometimes spoke at street meetings. Again I had a picture of him, standing bareheaded in the drizzle on Western Avenue, holding out his big square hands and promising that in the coming revolution the poor would inherit the earth.

The Swedish donkey-man I dubbed "a Puget Sound roustabout." He was methodical and self-contained, except for one angry encounter with the cook. We had finally crept into Spruce Inlet, about thirty miles south of Juneau, in the long northern twilight and tied up to a wharf beside a sawmill. Out in the harbor was our twin, the four-masted *Skykomish,* with a high deckload of lumber. We were to transfer to the laden vessel, leaving the *Snohomish* to be loaded by some Indians with the help of the donkey engine.

Before leaving the *Snohomish* we had to rig the cargo gaff for loading, and it took longer than we expected. When we finished, Donkey was hungry. Out of the galley came the cook, transformed in his hat and overcoat and carrying a straw suitcase. He had locked up the pantry and was ready to board the other vessel. But Donkey demanded food. He threatened the cook with a piece of hatch batten, and

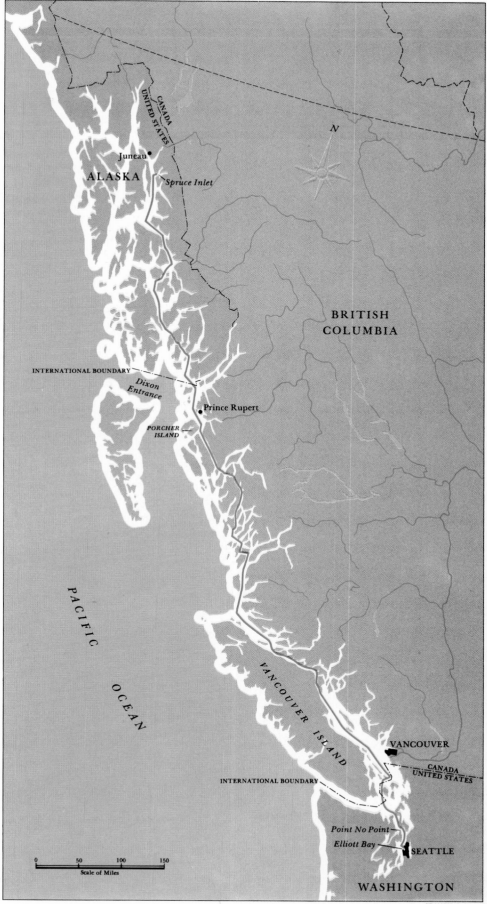

FRANCIS & SHAW

The bold red line traces the Inside Passage route between Seattle and Spruce Inlet in Alaska, taken by the author aboard old four-masters more than a half century ago.

Frenchy stepped back into the galley for a bread knife. It was a cat-and-dog fight, all snarling and spitting. Frenchy won, as usual. We went ashore to the Northern Lights Café, the only night spot in that one-street town, and ate sandwiches and pie with the tide slapping at pilings under the floor. The only Alaska towns I saw were built on tideland at the foot of sheer mountains. There were no roads to these coastal towns; each one was like an island.

When we left the Northern Lights, the twilight was gone and stars glimmered in the dark still water. The *Coutli* had gone whistling off somewhere to load bunker coal. We got our gear and pulled off in a skiff manned by a silent Indian. It was unaccountably impressive, oars creaking, cigarettes glowing in the dark, a few lights showing the lost little town, and from somewhere the steady roar of a waterfall. No one said a word while we crossed the black harbor and groped along the schooner's bow. With seabags on our shoulders we climbed a rope ladder onto the deckload.

The fo'c's'le, buried in lumber, was like a cave. We stumbled down the makeshift stairs, our feet loud in the ship's stillness, and found a lantern hanging from the foremast. Gibbs struck another match and turned up the flame. As we peered around, something stirred in a corner bunk and a low voice said, "Cheero, mates. Give us a cigarette?"

We had a stowaway. He was from Glasgow, he said, by way of Montreal, Whitehorse, and Skagway, and he wanted to get into the States. He had lost his "papers" in Juneau and had bribed an Indian to put him aboard our schooner after she was loaded. I wondered how he had got to that blind inlet and why he chose such a slow passage to the U.S.A. Actually it was a shrewd choice. The U.S. Customs had never searched a lumber barge at the end of a towline.

Next morning the *Coutli* came, with Captain Olson aboard. We hauled up some pantry stores and took the towline. The tugboat's whistle saluted the encircling mountains, and we started homeward. From shore came the snarl of the sawmill and the snorting of the steam engine. The first slingloads of lumber dropped into the *Snohomish*'s hold. A month later the empty *Sky-komish* would arrive back at Spruce Inlet, and the laden *Snohomish* would tie on to the tugboat.

The *Skykomish*, with her deckhouses walled in lumber, was more somber than the *Snohomish*, and the laden schooner moved more slowly than the light one. We were not a happy crew. Four men could not combat the gloom of that creaking old vessel. We had no jokes, disputes, quarrels, or arguments, no card or crap games. We never raised our voices. But we had a refugee, and that drew us together.

Our stowaway called himself Mc-Killan; we called him Sandy. He was a small, quick-moving, watchful man, perhaps twenty-five, with narrow eyes and a stubble of blond beard. There must have been some hazard behind him, but he never spoke of it. To keep out of sight of the cook and the captain he lay in his bunk all day. At night he paced the deckload like a prisoner. At first we resented him, an intruder in our gloomy fo'c's'le, but he soon became our common cause. We shared our meals with him, gave him cigarettes, told him when to crawl out of his hole and when to keep under cover.

One night, off Porcher Point near Prince Rupert, our towline parted in the tide-swept channel. We shouted, but our voices were lost in the mist. The *Coutli* kept going, straight for Seattle, and we were drifting toward the reef. At that excitement Sandy came across the deckload. "What's up, mates?" he asked.

"Lost our line," I began, when Gibbs warned: "Get out of sight, Mac. Here comes the Old Man."

Sandy ducked into the pilothouse, where I was tugging at the heavy wheel. Captain Olson came to the doorway. "Ring that bell," he said without looking in. "Keep ringing!" He went forward while I yanked the bell cord.

Ahead of us the *Coutli* swung around, her whistle banking off the mountains. She churned alongside of us, and a line slapped across the deck-load. While they fumbled for it Sandy stepped outside. Spraying a flashlight past him, Captain Olson said, "God damn it, Slim, get back on that wheel." Sandy slipped in beside me while they hauled up the new hawser and snubbed it around the foremast. (Our bollards were buried under ten feet of lumber.) With a short whistle blast the tugboat took a strain on the line, pointing us away from Porcher Ledge. We were under way when the fog closed in. Then the *Coutli* slowed to half speed, and Sandy crawled back into the buried fo'c's'le.

On the last morning, with the hills of Seattle looming through the rain, Donkey brought him a bucket of shaving water, and Rowley, who had forgot the gold of Siberia, offered him a partnership: they could get an old trawler and smuggle Chinese into the States from Vancouver at fifty dollars a head. Sandy agreed that was a good deal, but he had other fish to fry. He just wanted to get ashore in the States.

Crossing Elliott Bay we made our plans. One of us would keep watch on the captain, another on the cook, another at the gangway, and the fourth would give him the word when the coast was clear. Sandy would be the first man off. So we ate our last meal together, triumphant over the Immigration Service. Gibbs said that in the new society men would not be enclosed by artificial barriers.

Now in 1974, with jets flying far above the tiderips and the little tide-washed towns, the Top o' the World is just next door. But we had been to remote places, a long time on the way. In the Connecticut Street basin the *Coutli* shortened up the towline and eased us to the dock. We cast off the hawser, and they gave us a long blast of the whistle. It echoed from Alki Point, my log says, telling the world that we were back from a far country.

Walter Havighurst, a retired professor of English who lives in Oxford, Ohio, is the author of a book on prominent Ohioans that will be published this spring by G. P. Putnam's Sons. The Seattle waterfront was the scene of his first novel, Pier 17, *which appeared in 1935.*

Poisoned Darts from Cupid's Quiver

We tend to think of the turn of the century as a sentimental era when grown men were not ashamed to weep over music-hall effusions about motherhood and infant mortality. If ever there was an age that should have paid proper respect to St. Valentine's Day, it was this one. Therefore there is something faintly shocking about the perverse sideline on the following pages. They are valentines, they cost only a penny each, and they made many people unhappy once a year for more than a century. Comic valentines appeared in America as early as the 1820's, and by 1840 they were being produced on a large scale. The dubious art form reached its peak in the late nineties and early 1900's with the crude, vigorous examples shown here. The sketches attacked such vanished enemies of society as the stingy boarding-house keeper, as well as some that are still with us—the crooked policeman and the foul-mouthed teamster, for instance. After the 1920's the tone of the missives softened, and although insulting valentines are still manufactured, the ferocious broadsides on these pages have gone the way of the mandolin, the detachable cuff, the philosophy of Elbert Hubbard, and other turn-of-the-century miseries.

THESE VALENTINES ARE FROM THE COLLECTION OF ALBERT NEWTON

UNRELIABLE POLICEMAN.

You sneaking, worthless rascal, it's a shame you have a place
On the force of public guardians, with such a thievish face!
You are well paid, scurvy loafer, for the work you ought to do,
But to earn your pay is something that we can't expect from you.
No other cop at shirking is able to come nigh you,
And any one that wants to with a bowl of beer can buy you.

GETTING READY FOR THE BOARDERS

Preparing for the boarders!—Poor victims, what a feast
Will confront them when the sun displays his features in the east:
With what grim determination they will have to face their meal,
And how they will be longing that their jaws were made of steel!

HEAD OF THE HOUSE?

To bridle and bit you meekly submit,
    Like a horse that's been trained to obey—
A horse? no an ass would be more in your class,
    Such a lack of all spunk you display.

YOUR PIPE-DREAM

To capture the boss, designing Miss,
Is your fantastic dream of bliss.
That you will trap him, I much doubt—
The chances are he'll fire you out.

MRS. OVERDRESS

Your poor old husband slaves all day
To dress you in this silly way.
But, worse and worse, each year, you get,
While he gets deeper into debt.

SLOW SUICIDE

If health and strength a man would lose,
One certain means there is to choose---
Inhale the cigarette's deadly smoke,
And prematurely he will croak.

ALCOHOL IS GETTING IN ITS WORK

A man transformed to a reptile!
A direful change that would be:
But in you the Booze demon is working
A change as dreadful to see.

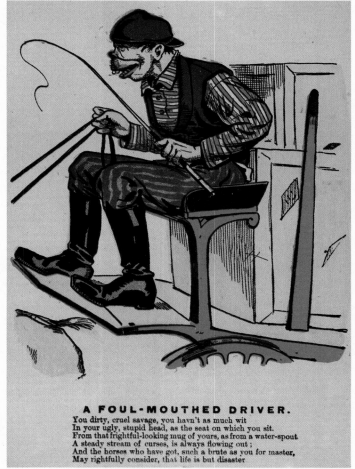

A FOUL-MOUTHED DRIVER.

You dirty, cruel savage, you havn't as much wit
In your ugly, stupid head, as the seat on which you sit.
From that frightful-looking mug of yours, as from a water-spout
A steady stream of curses, is always flowing out ;
And the horses who have got, such a brute as you for master,
May rightfully consider, that life is but disaster

The dignified portrait, opposite, of Bear's Belly, an Arikara Indian warrior of the eastern plains, wrapped in a bearskin, the symbol of his personal medicine—and the photographs of the other native Americans on the following pages—are a sampling of a wondrous, but almost unknown, publishing project that took one dedicated photographer-author, Edward S. Curtis—sometimes directing a staff of up to sixty assistants—thirty years to complete and that the spellbound New York *Herald* called in 1907, when Curtis' first illustrated volumes began to appear, "the most gigantic in the making of books since the King James edition of the Bible. . . ."

Edward Curtis in the field

The Splendid Indians of
EDWARD S. CURTIS

The result of a singularly lucky stroke that brought together the odd combination of a talented photographer, President Theodore Roosevelt, and the financial giant J. Pierpont Morgan, and did it at the last possible moment when Indians could be photographed as they were before their lives were altered by white men, Curtis' huge work consisted of twenty sumptuous volumes of text and hand-printed, sepia-toned photogravures, each one accompanied by a portfolio of thirty-six or more large photogravures printed, also by hand, on 18″ × 22″ sheets. Titled collectively *The North American Indian* and containing a total of more than two thousand stunning photographs of some eighty different tribes, the forty volumes and portfolios were issued over a twenty-three-year period, from 1907 to 1930. They were sold to subscribers at a price that averaged $3,500 a set, depending upon the method of payment. Curtis' original plan was to publish five hundred sets, but he sold only two hundred fourteen of them and limited his printing to that number of sets. Today they are highly prized collector's items, reposing principally in the rare-book rooms of libraries and little known to the general public. When occasionally they appear at auctions, they bring prices in the neighborhood of $35,000 a set, and even individual prints sometimes sell for several

TEXT CONTINUES ON PAGE 57

By ALVIN M. JOSEPHY, JR.

40

Hopi women posed on the roofs of their adobe homes for this scene in 1921.

Inside their tepee Curtis photographed this proud Piegan chief and his son.

Curtis began his grand project in 1900, when he visited a Piegan camp in northern Montana and took pictures of a Plains tribe's traditional style of living, typified by their great circle of tepees, below. Fifty years earlier, the Piegans, one of the Blackfoot tribes, had been among the most feared warriors on the plains; by the time Curtis saw them, troops, starvation, and disease caught from the white man had crushed them.

OVERLEAF: *The Atsina, once a warlike tribe allied with the Blackfeet, were among the friendliest Plains Indians he photographed, according to Curtis. His request in 1908 that they don their old war garb and sit with feathered lances for this idealized version of one of their war parties of the past probably pleased them with memories of happier, prereservation days, when they were free to hunt buffalo and fight their enemies.*

With patience and tact, Curtis was able to picture many ceremonies and rites rarely seen, much less photographed, by white men. Among them was a masked dance of Kwakiutls of British Columbia, two participants of which are seen, left, enacting the roles of long-beaked bird servants of a mythical monster, and a solemn medicine ceremony of Arikara Indians, below.

A Kwakiutl endowed with a wasp's spirit
Kwakiutl blanket and anthropomorphic mask

A Koskimo dance garb from Vancouver Island
"Bringer of confusion," a Koskimo spirit

Curtis was fascinated by the artistry of the masks and costumes used by numerous tribes in their relationships with the supernatural world.
Many, like those seen here, were destroyed by white missionaries, educators, and government agents, who strove, according to their lights, to
suppress Indian religions, mythology, and lore as superstitious, until the Indians—and all the world—lost a rich and inspiring heritage.

Sisiutl, a Kwakiutl double-headed snake

A striking Kwakiutl "man of the sea" mask

Kwakiutl mask, reminiscent of the Chinese

A Nunivak Eskimo and his mask in Alaska

A Navaho spiritual mask from the Southwest

Curtis' photographs of Indian women show them as proud and dignified as the men. The Mohave girl from the lower Colorado River, left, was named Mosa, and Curtis said, "She had the eyes of a fawn as it emerges from the forest, questioning all the strange sights, sounds and colors of civilization." The Wishram Indian girl, below, was from the area of The Dalles on the Columbia River. For her picture in 1910, she put on all her finery, including a beaded deerskin dress, strands of shell beads, dentalium-shell nose and ear ornaments, and a headdress of beads, shells, and Chinese coins acquired by her ancestors from sea traders. Children, too, were the subject of many of Curtis' pictures. At right is an Apache baby on an Arizona reservation in 1903, tied against the hooded board by which his mother carried him on her back.

Yakotlus, a whiskered Kwakiutl

Spotted Bull, a Mandan

Two Whistles, a Mountain Crow

Contrary to popular opinion, Indian physical features vary greatly, reflecting the backgrounds of peoples who entered North America from Asia at different times and evolved separately in the Western Hemisphere. The Piegan man, Iron Breast, above, and the Cheyenne, Porcupine, left, in a sunshade of cottonwood leaves, were Algonquin, as different from Kwakiutls and Crows as Scots from, say, Italians and Poles.

Along the forested Pacific coast of the Northwest and in the deserts of the South-west, where whites had not yet penetrated in great numbers, Curtis was able to photo-graph centuries-old customs that would soon change or disappear. At left, on the British Columbia coast, is a Kwakiutl wedding party in large painted canoes made from single trees. Below is a Hopi girl of Arizona in traditional bridal garb, 1900.

hundred dollars each if in good condition.

Curtis, who was born on a farm near Whitewater, Wisconsin, in 1868, was something of a driven man, convinced early in life that the Indians were a vanishing people and determined that he would publish a set of books recording with text and pictures their customs in peace and war, their ceremonies, and their religious observances. His ambitious undertaking, requiring years of arduous field research and photographic trips, heavy costs for supplies, printing, and publishing—not to mention a livelihood for himself, his family, and his assistants—faced disaster many times; and in the end he collapsed with a mental and physical breakdown that put him in the hospital for two years. But by fanatic perseverance he accomplished his goal, taking some forty thousand pictures of almost every tribe in Alaska and the trans-Mississippi West between 1898 and 1930 and compiling a monumental record of the aboriginal people as they were before their own way of life disappeared or changed. Yet while the enormous ethnological importance of

A limited edition of the entire set of Curtis gravures, as well as individual copies taken from the original plates of those appearing in this portfolio, are available to AMERICAN HERITAGE subscribers. Information on either the sets or individual gravures may be obtained by writing to Mr. Martin Rapp, American Heritage Publishing Company, Inc., 1221 Avenue of the Americas, New York City, New York 10020.

Curtis' work and the breathtaking quality of his photography place him in the first rank of those who captured the image of the unconquered Indian, he himself has remained as little known as his magnificent books. It is ironic that toward the end of his life, with his Indian volumes already published, he worked in relative obscurity in such jobs as still cameraman in Hollywood on the set of Cecil B. De Mille's *Ten Commandments*.

Curtis' photography of Indians began soon after he first arrived at Puget Sound from Wisconsin in 1887, when he was nineteen. In the Midwest he had already learned the photographer's trade. Fascinated by a stereopticon given him when he was a boy by his father, a Civil War veteran and minister in the United Brethren Church, and inspired by a book on photography, he had built his own camera, using two wooden boxes and the stereo lenses. In time he landed a job in a St. Paul photographic gallery, working in a darkroom and taking commercial pictures. When his father fell ill and the family migrated to the milder climate of Washington Territory, Edward went along and helped

The regal portrait opposite is of a Kwakiutl chief's daughter, wrapped in her cedar-bark rain cape and supported on carved images of her slaves. Almost uniquely among Indians, the Northwest coast tribes were divided into classes of nobility, commoners, and slaves and venerated the acquisition of private possessions.

build a log cabin in what was still sparsely settled country across Puget Sound from Seattle.

His father died soon after the move, and Edward, one of four brothers and sisters, became the chief breadwinner, taking odd jobs like the others but also buying a good camera and bringing in money from his photography. There were many picturesque subjects in the area—the mountains and dense forests, still almost wilderness, the new settlements in the Washington valleys, and the shipping in Puget Sound. But there were also many Indians, survivors of numerous coastal tribes, and Curtis was drawn more and more to them as subjects, paying them a dollar or so to pose for portraits and photographing them as they fished, trapped, and hunted seals in the harbors. Less than forty years before, he recognized, these Indians had been the proud, free owners of the region. Then they were crushed, forced to cede their lands, and overrun and debauched by white society. As he photographed them he imagined what they had been like before the white man came. Although theirs was now a life of poverty, sickness, alcoholism, and helplessness—the demoralized plight of what most people of the time considered a vanishing race—Curtis increasingly tried to idealize them, to picture them as they might have looked in the past. Taking great pains with the poses, settings, expressive actions, and dress and ornamentation of his subjects and making sure, as he once explained, that no sign of white civilization crept into his shots, he strove for an evocative quality that would convey the original dignity and humanity of the tribesmen. In addition, to heighten the dramatic mood he frequently retouched his negatives, printing them with a soft and fuzzy tone that eliminated many background details. The net effect, of course, was a misrepresentation of reality, but this did not bother him.

His Indian pictures, displayed and sold in a Seattle photograph store, soon became very popular, and several of them, entered in contests and photographic exhibitions that toured the United States and Europe, won prizes and medals. In 1892 he married and, with a hundred fifty dollars of borrowed money, bought a partnership in a Seattle studio. Two years later he became sole owner, continuing to photograph local Indians but also catering to the market for scenic views of the Northwest. Becoming a skilled mountaineer in the process, he photographed the peaks of the Cascades, particularly Mount Rainier. There, in 1898, he came upon a lost party and guided it to safety.

It proved to be a turning point in his life. Among the group he rescued were several nationally prominent persons, including Gifford Pinchot, chief of the United States Forest Service, Dr. C. Hart Merriam, chief of the United States Biological Survey, and George Bird Grinnell, editor of *Forest and Stream* magazine and a well-known naturalist and writer on the Blackfoot Indians.

Grinnell and Curtis became good friends, and the following year Grinnell, who was greatly impressed by Curtis' Indian photographs, invited him to accompany a two-month exploring expedition by ship along the Alaskan coast, organized and financed by E. H. Harriman, the railroad tycoon. It was a boatload of famous men. Among the passengers were John Muir, who was then studying glaciers, John Burroughs, the ornithologist and author, and Henry Gannett of the United States Geological Survey. Curtis, the chief photographer, had an opportunity to widen his circle of influential friends and with an assistant, D. G. Inverarity of Seattle, took more than five thousand photographs.

When it was over, Grinnell invited him on another excursion the next year, this time on a visit for two weeks to the Piegan Indians, one of the Blackfoot tribes, in northern Montana. Grinnell's friendship with the Indians permitted the two men to observe the sacred ceremony of the sun dance, as well as intimate details of tribal daily life. The experience made an enormous impact on Curtis and inspired the project that was to occupy him for the next thirty years. Unlike the crushed and dispossessed Indians around Puget Sound, the Piegans, he noted, still retained a large measure of their original culture. What he and Grinnell had been privileged to view, he felt, was known to few white men and would soon be gone.

He broached his idea to Grinnell—to visit every tribe in the West, studying and photographing them and publishing their histories with pictures and text that he would write. The project, he estimated, would take five or six years of his own and an assistant's time, might cost as much as $25,000, and could be financed by sales of his pictures and of the finished sets of perhaps several volumes. When he was done, he told Grinnell, he would have a lasting record of the "Indian as he was in his normal, noble life so people will know he was no debauched vagabond but a man of proud stature and noble heritage." Grinnell responded enthusiastically to the proposal, gave Curtis a short course in the kinds of questions to ask and information to gather among the tribes, and assured him of his support in making his work known to others.

Curtis was off almost immediately, like a man possessed. Within ten days, after a brief stop in Seattle, where he put his studio affairs in the hands of associates, he was on the Hopi reservation in Arizona, commencing to photograph as if he feared that the other tribes would disappear before he could get to them. After the Hopis he moved through the Arizona desert and along the Gila and Colorado rivers, photographing the Navahos, Apaches, Mohaves, and other southwestern tribes. From time to time, between 1900 and 1904, he returned to Seattle with his glass-plate negatives, making and selling prints to keep himself going, then hurrying off to photograph more tribes.

It was a grueling, committed life, full of frustrations, difficulties, and hardships in the field; but, as Curtis later said, he thought of himself as a man with a mission whose time was running out. Tall, rugged, and husky, still in his thirties, he was generally able to maintain good health as he drove his rattling photographic wagon across the reservations, through all kinds of terrain and climate, visiting remote villages, hunting camps, fishing stations, and sacred sites. He lived in the deserts, the mountains, the open plains, and the deep forests. Sometimes there were no roads, and he had to travel by packhorse. He started with a 14″ × 17″ box camera with a fine German lens, but it was big and cumbersome, and he switched eventually to an 11 × 14, and finally to a 6 × 8, reflex camera. He used a tripod and natural lighting for all of his pictures and took most of his portraits of Indians in his tent, which was lined with a maroon-colored drape and had a skylight on one side, with a curtain to control the light. Almost all of his pictures were taken on glass plates that were heavy, fragile, and hard to handle in the field; he carried them in trunks and changed them into their holders in a changing bag or in his tent at night.

Curtis started with relatively little knowledge of Indian history or culture, and his early attitudes reflected the white man's conventional point of view about them. He referred to the Hopis' religious beliefs as "superstitious" and their sacred rites and ceremonies as "esoteric." He was sometimes frustrated by headmen in getting the pictures he wanted and said there was no use arguing with them, for "Indian logic is apart from the American's." But he was becoming a good student of human nature and developing increasing patience, diplomacy, and, above all, a growing understanding of the Indian's point of view about himself and about all white men. They recognized his genuine sympathy and helped him secure the pictures and historic and cultural information he wanted.

It was rarely easy to tell Indians what to wear and where and how to pose and, in addition, to ply them with questions about their religious beliefs and other secret and personal details. But by trial and error Curtis learned how to win over most of his subjects. Sometimes he gained acceptance through the help of a paid interpreter or a missionary or a government agent. At other times he got what he wanted by simply paying the Indians or buying them a meal. He learned to practice guile and go through long periods of patient waiting, during which he did his best to seem uninterested and "innocent," until gradually he won friendship and confidence. Seemingly idle conversation about nature, he found, would attract an Indian's curiosity and lead him to talk about other things. Once, to get Apache shamans to reveal the secrets of their religious life, he spent days assuming a "nonchalant indifference." In time he found himself being accepted. Presently he paid some of the Apaches to take trips with him in the mountains. More and more people—men, women, and children, and finally shamans—came along. "Had the medicine men dreamed," he said, "that I possessed a real questioning thought, nothing could have induced them to join the party. But no—I was just a sucker furnishing the food and paying for the privilege." At last, totally trusting him, the shamans "went on with their devotions," oblivious to the white man who was carefully watching. The final step, taking the pictures, required only a bit more time.

Late in the fall of 1904 Curtis took stock of his situation and realized that he was far from achieving his goal. There were still many more tribes unvisited than visited, and he had not started on his books. He was running out of money. He returned to Seattle and placed some of his best pictures on public exhibition, but the acclaim they received in the newspapers and from the public did not solve his problem. With the aid of some of his influential friends in the East, including E. H. Harriman, Pinchot, and Grinnell, who published a flattering article about his work, he arranged for a series of exhibits and lectures on Indians in Washington, D.C. There Curtis came to the White House to photograph Geronimo, who had been brought to the national capital to participate in Theodore Roosevelt's inauguration, and the photographer was then presented to the President. Roosevelt admired his work greatly and urged him to continue with it. But still there was no money, and Curtis spent most of the rest of the year lecturing at exhibits of his photographs in a half dozen cities from Boston to Portland, Oregon, and selling prints merely to pay his expenses.

By November he realized that without the help of a wealthy patron he could not go on with his project. Roosevelt's interest in his pictures gave him an idea, and rather desperately Curtis wrote to him seeking advice and a testimonial that might help him raise funds. The President replied on December 18, 1905, providing Curtis with a laudatory letter that he could use "in talking with any man who has any interest in the subject." The President's response, praising Curtis for engaging in "one of the most valuable works which any American could now do," gave him a lift and encouraged him toward his next step. On January 24, 1906, undoubtedly as a result of his use of Roosevelt's letter, he received an appointment on Wall Street with the nation's most powerful financier, J. Pierpont Morgan the Elder.

The meeting was a success. After showing Morgan a portfolio of his prints Curtis won from him a grant of $15,000 a year for five years to be used for his field expenses. The two men agreed that the first of the books would be published as soon as possible in a limited, finely printed and bound edition of five hundred copies, that each book would be accompanied by a large-sized portfolio of Curtis' prints, and that Morgan would receive twenty-five sets for himself. The high subscription price of three thousand dollars a set, Morgan estimated, would more than meet the publishing costs.

Buoyed by his good fortune, Curtis hurried back to the field with plans to have his first two volumes in the hands of the printer within a year. Aided by a number of assistants, including a skilled stenographer who took down in rapid shorthand an interpreter's version of the Indians' replies to his questions, Curtis travelled rapidly from one reservation to the next in the Southwest, completing his research. In the winter of 1906–7 he and his assistants settled down in a hideaway for three months to prepare the text for publication. "Our regular working hours during these months were from eight in the morning until one the next morning, seven days a week," he later wrote. Even his family did not know where he was, and there were no interruptions.

The text, a mixture of ethnological material, Indian history, reminiscences, biography, and lore, as well as Curtis' accounts of his photographic adventures, was not, as might be expected, the work of a trained scientist. But it was filled with informative material gathered by no one else, and much of it, particularly the narratives of older Indians, would have a lasting value. Finished in the spring of 1907, it was taken to the printer in Boston by one of Curtis' assistants, who remained in the East to oversee publication while Curtis returned to the field with an even larger party than before, completing research among the Sioux and other Plains tribes for Volumes III and IV. The first two books and their portfolios, dealing with the Apaches, Navahos, and other tribes of the Southwest, came off the press in December, 1907, and were sent to those who had already subscribed for the set.

The books, printed by the University Press of Cambridge, with soft, sepia photogravures hand printed from copperplates by John Andrew and Son in Boston, were as luxurious as advertised. The volumes contained some three hundred fifty quarto pages, measuring $9\frac{1}{2}'' \times 12\frac{1}{2}''$, printed on two different handmade papers of the highest and most expensive quality, one an imported Japanese vellum and the other a special Dutch etching stock, called Van Gelder, that heightened the rich feeling of the photographs. The binding was three-quarter levant with gold tops. The work itself was enhanced by the editing of Frederick Webb Hodge of the Bureau of American Ethnology in Washington, one of the nation's top recognized authorities on the Indian, who was then in the midst of

CONTINUED ON PAGE 96

BOURBON

amber waves of grain—100 proof

By GERALD CARSON

In the early years of this century, when an American scholar, James Schouler, could still define history as the record of "consecutive public events," it would have been inconceivable for the American contribution to the world's varieties of distilled spirits to be considered a proper subject of academic inquiry. But if one accepts the view prevailing among scholars today—that history includes the whole life of a people—then the manners and customs associated with bourbon (pronounced "ber-bun" in Kentucky, as in "urban") deserve a special chapter in our social chronicles.

Alcoholic liquors distilled from molasses and from rye appeared in America before bourbon, but sugar cane is a product of the West Indies, and rye is an Old World grain. On the other hand, true bourbon whiskey—distilled from our own native maize, given character by limestone water and yeasts from the salubrious air of the Bourbon Belt, cradled during a long slumber in barrels of charred white oak—can with accuracy be called the distinctive spirit of our country. Indeed it was formally recognized as such by Congress in Senate Concurrent Resolution 19, adopted on May 4, 1964.

Our own American beverage is intimately associated with valor and the graces of life, with villainy and folly, with dramatic events such as the Whiskey Rebellion, with national scandals such as the Whiskey Ring in Grant's administration (when revenue officers cheated their own agency), and with the fur trade and the opening of the Great West. Red liquor—often, it must be admitted, a cheap, colored liquor affectionately known as red-eye—accompanied the westering Americans in their conquest of a continent—the bullwhackers, traders, trappers, hide hunters, soldiers, sodbusters, gold seekers, and government surveyors. Ranchers, railroad contractors, United States marshals, and mountain men shared an opinion so

The humble origins of Kentucky whiskey were romanticized in the label on the barrelheads of Peach Orchard Bourbon in 1873.

favorable toward native whiskey in general that Mark Twain once suggested that the line stamped on the back cover of George Bancroft's *History of the United States*—"Westward the star of empire takes its way"—would better reflect the American experience if rendered "Westward the jug of empire takes its way."

Whiskey and government are yoked together in an intimate relationship derived from the power of Congress to levy taxes and the fact that it takes a powerful lot of sour-mash bourbon to run the government in a big country like the United States. The role of liquor along the Potomac has long been hailed by social commentators.

"Whiskey is the best part of the American government," declared Achille Murat, son of the king of Naples, who married a great-grandniece of George Washington and wrote three friendly but candid books about the United States.

Today the seat of our national government drinks about seven times as much straight bourbon per capita as the national average and about four times the gallonage required to slake the legal thirst of Kentucky. Such liberal use of ardent spirits is not a recent development. The Supreme Court under Chief Justice John Marshall developed a rule that its members would take a drink only in rainy weather. That was interpreted to include any rain that fell within the Court's jurisdiction. And it was further stipulated that there was always rain falling somewhere in the continental United States. Mrs. Anne Royall, a shrewd observer of life and customs in the United States, wrote early in the nineteenth century, when the Capitol was under construction, that of some two hundred men employed on the job not more than six were sober. And she reported that whiskey was sold by the drink in the passage between the Senate chamber and the House by persons she described as "abandoned females."

One of the earliest known whiskey brands was Sterne's Celebrated Congress Bourbon, named in compliment to our national legislature. The label showed a picture of the House of Representatives in session in the old chamber, now known as the Hall of Statuary. Until the early nineteen hundreds there was a damp spot, known as the hole in the wall, in either end of the Capitol for the convenience of the members of Congress whose custom it was to drink water after pouring whiskey of native growth into it.

There is a political theory that has long been nourished on the Republican side of the House that there is a special affinity between whiskey and Democrats. It is reflected in an old remark: "I never said all Democrats were saloonkeepers. What I did say

The best is none too good for us.

"ROYAL VELVET" WHISK

Three turn-of-the-century examples of soft sell: Kentucky Dew claimed to be the "Standard of Purity," thus outraging the W.C.T.U. *Big Spring dared associate itself with an intoxicatingly naked lady. Royal Velvet took the view that bourbon was a part of growing up.*

was that all saloonkeepers are Democrats." During an agonizing debate in 1880 on whether the excise tax should be forgiven on the whiskey that evaporated during the aging period—amounting to a substantial 36 per cent in eight years—Hiram Casey Young, a Tennessee Democrat, rose in the House to say:

Forming my opinion from frequent declarations of my Republican friends, I had concluded, before the commencement of the discussion which has been had upon this bill, that the subject of whiskey was peculiarly under the charge of the Democratic party. . . . But it must be admitted, I think, that Republican gentlemen have in the discussion evinced an acquaintance with the subject so thorough and intimate that it could hardly have been acquired otherwise than by the closest relations.

To this salty observation the *Congressional Record* appends the stage direction *laughter and applause*. Omar Dwight Conger, a Michigan Republican, then replied that any familiarity he had with whiskey was due to the many years he had spent in close association with Democrats. "If I have not been able to feel their influence," he said, "I have certainly smelt their breath."

The best evidence is that the pleasures of sipping our star-spangled juice of the corn plant do cross party lines. Colonel Robert G. Ingersoll, the silver-tongued Republican orator from Peoria, called bourbon "liquid joy" that has spent, as he put it in the flowery language of nineteenth-century eloquence, "the dreamy tawny dusks of many perfect days . . . within the happy staves of oak."

The inviting bottle, when circulated in the inner councils of the House leaders at sundown, has the reputation of being an effective aid in smoothing the way for legislation and assessing the temper of the members. The usefulness of the bourbon-and-branch-water ritual was also demonstrated in the Senate when, its presiding officer, Vice President John Nance "Cactus Jack" Garner, proposed to his colleagues, at about the time of the Children's Hour, that they lay aside the cares of statesmanship and, as he put it, "strike a blow for liberty." No less

distinguished an authority upon history, government, and bourbon than the late award-winning historian Bernard DeVoto has maintained that bourbon whiskey, taken without ice by American patriots, quickens the political processes, disperses doubts and shadows, and helps men of good will to resolve their differences.

No one knows how primitive man became acquainted with alcohol. Far back in prehistory some gifted individual must have observed a mess of fruits or berries spoiling in a watery solution. He must have tasted the liquid and found that it made the world seem a wonderful place. Anthropologists have conjectured that alcohol created the first agriculture as our nomadic ancestors settled down to cultivate the vine. Stronger beverages than fermentation provides arrived with the invention of the alembic, or still. From a mash of fermented grain or fruit pulp placed in the still, alcohol was vaporized by direct heat, separated from the water because of differing boiling points, cooled, and caught again in a condensing coil—a raw distillate, colorless as water and searing in its effect.

The first ardent spirits distilled in English-speaking America were fruit cordials and brandies. The native grape was not well adapted for making wine or brandy. But apple trees flourished mightily and were common in New England from the seventeenth century on, and so was cider, meaning hard cider, which was distilled into apple brandy or applejack. John Adams took a tankard of hard cider as his morning phlegm-cutter and kept eight or ten barrels in the cellar. Dr. Edward Augustus Holyoke, Harvard, class of 1746, who was awarded the college's first degree of doctor of medicine, mixed his cider with rum, took a half pint with some water at dinner, another with his pipe afterward, and became the first Harvard man to live to be a hundred. It was apple brandy that men called upon to help them build the famous stone walls of New England. According to folk tradition, it took a gallon of apple

brandy to lay up a rod of wall.

The most important spiritous liquor during the eighteenth century was rum, first known as rumbullion, a term of unknown origin. A field hand expected a gallon a month as part of his wages. Daily liquor rations were issued in the regular army until 1830, and a man who was elected an officer at the militia trainings was expected to wet his commission bountifully with Medford rum or good old Demerara. The customer in a country store expected after a substantial purchase to get a complimentary glass from the

GLASS CONTAINER MANUFACTURERS INSTITUTE

friendly rural merchant.

The Revolutionary War years mark the beginning of rum's decline. Among the reasons for this were the steady shift of the center of population to the westward and the arrival of the Scotch-Irish, a self-reliant people who were traditionally grain distillers and crossed the Alleghenies lugging their shining copper stills with them. Rye was already prospering in the western parts of both Maryland and Pennsylvania in the late eighteenth century, and the corn was growing tall in Kentucky. The distillation of corn whiskey, a colorless, unaged liquor that may be called bourbon's country cousin, was simply a way of marketing the frontier grain crop, reducing its weight and bulk and enhancing its value. A pack horse could move only four bushels of grain. But it could carry the equivalent of twenty-four bushels if they were condensed into two kegs of whiskey slung across its back, while the value of the goods would double when they reached the eastern markets. So whiskey became the remittance from the fringe settlements for the necessities of life. The Whiskey Rebellion in the 1790's was a mass protest against the levy of a tax by the United States on the farm whiskey of Pennsylvania and Kentucky. The hated tax was quietly re-

that for two generations Americans could lift a horn of "bald face" without feeling that they were helping to pay off the national debt.

This was the period when Whig gentlemen in broadcloth raised their tall hats reverently if Mr. Clay's name was mentioned, when whiskey came in barrels, and when loyal consumers carried their own personal flasks, hand-blown in delightful designs reflecting the topical interests of the day. The flasks carried such mottoes as "Corn for the World," "Success to the Railroads," or General Zachary

titudes after the temperance movement picked up speed, and the fact that distilling was not an industrial activity but simply a part-time adjunct of agriculture. In fact, a common term for the product was "country whiskey." It was distilled from maize, to be sure, but collected just as it dripped from the condensing coil. The first known advertisement in which the term "bourbon whiskey" appeared was published in 1821. But the distillate of the period was not bourbon as defined today, since it lacked the bouquet and reddish color as well as the smoothness produced by proper aging in charred oak cooperage.

Bourbon as a place name in Kentucky occurs for the same reason that one finds such other names of French reference as Paris, Louisville, Versailles, and Fayette, and for the same reason that Vergennes, Vermont, commemorates the name of the foreign minister of Louis XVI—that is, gratitude for French assistance in the American War of Independence. Enthusiastic claims have been advanced for various counties in the bluegrass region as the exact spot where bourbon originated. Senator Garret Davis, for example, told the United States Senate in 1862, "The liquor that is termed 'old Bourbon' had its origin in the county in which I reside. . . ." Senator Davis was undoubtedly right if he meant simply to apply the term "old Bourbon" to a general geographic region, since Bourbon County, which was carved out of Fayette County in 1785, included all or part of thirty-four of the present-day counties in eastern Kentucky. Oddly enough, Bourbon County now produces no bourbon.

Colonel Edmund Haynes Taylor, Jr., a grandnephew of Zachary Taylor and creator of the still well-regarded brand known as Old Taylor, once insisted that bourbon originated in the year of the Declaration of Independence and would endure as long as the liberties set forth in that proclamation. The James E. Pepper family, another distiller, promoted the same idea by adopting the slogan "Born with the Republic." But these and many other charming legends of similar import cannot be substantiated. It is safer to

The ad above would seem to prove the old Republican claim of an affinity between Democrats and whiskey. At Churchill Downs about 1893, taking their bourbon straight, are, left to right, Treasury Secretary John G. Carlisle, Senator Joseph C. S. Blackburn, and ex-Governor J. Proctor Knott, all Kentucky Democrats, with John G. Roach, a distiller. Left: Washington flask, ca. 1840.

pealed in 1802 during Jefferson's administration. But in the meantime some two thousand frontiersmen had floated downriver from Redstone Old Fort (later Brownsville) to Kentucky with their burr mills and copper stills to cultivate a corn patch and set up their furnaces once more. The federal tax on alcoholic beverages was revived briefly during the War of 1812. After

Taylor's reputed order to young artillery officer Braxton Bragg at a desperate moment during the Battle of Buena Vista: "A little more grape, Captain Bragg." Portraits of Lafayette, Washington, and Old Rough and Ready appeared frequently on these personal flasks. In their writings on American glass the scholarly McKearins, George and Helen, observed, "To adorn common whisky bottles with the likeness of our great . . . did not belittle the man or the country in the eyes of the citizens who bought the flasks. . . ."

Information on the early history of whiskey in Kentucky is fragmentary. There are several reasons for this: the rugged conditions of life in a frontier state, the overlay of later moral at-

CONTINUED ON PAGE 95

A Last Glimpse of the Steamboats

Americans have always loved steam. We cannot claim the steam engine as our invention, but we did adopt it at once and brought it to the peak of its development. The device took on peculiarly American forms in this country; compare, for instance, the tidy British locomotives with their rangy American counterparts. So too with our steamboats. While they lacked the sharp beauty of the clippers, they made up for it with their powerful, chunky, intricate American grace. They plied our rivers and coastal waters for most of the last century, the lines vying with each other to produce ever grander, more luxuriously appointed ships. And they were grand, for they were a source of pride as well as income to their owners. As early as 1847 owner George Law, churning up the Hudson on his *Oregon*, ordered chairs, bunks, doors, and even wainscoting fed into the furnaces to avoid the terrible humiliation of losing a race to one of Cornelius Vanderbilt's ships.

Most of the steamboat men were of Law's cut. They were proud and arrogant and looked down on the railroads as crude, grimy transportation, useful only in getting travelers to the docks. Once aboard ship, the passengers could sleep in princely staterooms, stroll through vast "grand saloons," and eat lobster for fifty cents while they watched the lights of small towns ghosting by on the shore.

Throughout the first quarter of our own century the ships grew larger and more splendid, but they were doomed. Even at the height of their glory they were being forced out of commission by cheaper, lesser forms of transportation. Their fate is eloquently expressed in the painting on the opposite page. Here is the sidewheeler *Ida*, a victim of the Depression, mouldering by a weedy bank in Saugerties Creek, New York, through the dog days,

waiting for the wrecker's hammer. She was painted by William Gordon Muller, whose evocative views of American steamboats appear in the following portfolio.

Muller was six years old when he was first beguiled by a Hudson River Day Line sidewheeler gliding upriver with her flags flying and an orchestra playing on her deck. From then on the big ships were never far from his thoughts. By the time he was eighteen, Muller held the post of quartermaster on the Day Line steamer *Alexander Hamilton*, by then the last sidewheeler on the East Coast, now unhappily gone to join her sisters in retirement. Muller currently divides his time between acting as art director for an advertising agency and painting his scenes of the steamers in their heyday. "I take pride in painting my steamboats very accurately," says Muller, "drawing from a large collection of reference material and from knowledge gained firsthand from my involvement with some last members of the real thing."

But Muller's paintings are more than accurate representations. They can also serve to remind us that, as a people, we tend to be far too dedicated to destroying the remnants of our immediate past. The steamers with their long white hulls and huge walking beams were a vital and significant part of that past. But the big ships are gone, and they will not come back, and we can only echo the sentiments of Rudyard Kipling's mournful quatrain on the vanished Fall River Line:

> *No more I'll see the trawlers drift*
> *Below the Bass Rock ground,*
> *Or watch the tall Fall steamer lights*
> *Tear blazing up the Sound.*

A Portfolio of Paintings by William Gordon Muller

PHOTOGRAPHED BY JOHN CONBOY

*The **Priscilla**, flagship of the Fall River Line, slices through the rippled waters of Long Island Sound. With an overall length of 440 feet, she was the largest sidewheeler in the world when she was launched in 1894. Even when the line built a bigger vessel, the **Priscilla** kept her reputation as the finest ship on this famous waterway up to the time she was scrapped in 1938. Something of the delight she inspired is conveyed by an awed visitor, the Scottish writer David Christie Murray: "I sailed in her from New York before my acquaintance with America was twelve hours old, and she seemed to offer a sort of letter of credentials from this gigantic Republic to the visiting stranger."*

66

Below: This tough, ungainly little workhorse of 1916 outlived the sleek Priscilla *by thirty years. She is steam tug* #3, *owned by the New York Central Railroad, and she operated with the last fleet of steam tugs in New York Harbor until her retirement in the late 1960's.*

OVERLEAF: *The "Iron Monarch of Long Island Sound" leaves her berth in New York Harbor. The* Pilgrim, *launched in 1883, was the first iron-hulled steamer on the Fall River Line and the first American steamboat to make use of a double hull, a feature that saved her life when a rock ledge scraped open her bottom. The elegant ship was in service until 1913. Her decks were covered with $60,000 worth of carpets, and she was electrified from bow to stern, an achievement that was ecstatically hailed in an advertising brochure: "She is lighted with 1,000 incandescent electric lights . . . and Mr. Edison has exhausted his inventive faculties in fitting up this magnificent vessel."*

With her boilers cold and paddlewheels still, the massive **Hendrick Hudson** *is ignominiously nuzzled out of her berth by the tugboats that are to tow her on her last voyage. She was built for the Hudson River Day Line in 1906 and, in her day, had the largest passenger capacity of any river steamer in the world. Fifty-five hundred people could ride her in comfort, a record to be exceeded six years later by the Day Line's* Washington Irving, *licensed to carry six thousand. Six boilers fed the* Hudson's *engines, which pushed the massive ship up and down the Hudson River until the end of the traditional Day Line Company in 1948. The* Hendrick Hudson *was left to rust at her pier for three years and finally, under a lowering sky, was towed away to the wreckers at Tacone, Pennsylvania. Within the next few years all of the eastern sidewheelers would follow her into oblivion.*

THE RELIEF OF Fort Pickens

By JAMES COOLEY

The instrument of policy: Montgomery C. Meigs

WAR WAS DAYS AWAY, A UNION STRONGHOLD WAS THREATENED,

AND THROUGH A FOG OF RUMOR, DOUBT, CONTRADICTORY ORDERS,

AND OUTRIGHT LIES THE ARMY AND NAVY SET OUT TO HELP

A good place to start the story is the Republican convention in Chicago in May, 1860. By long odds the leading candidate, and on form and experience the best qualified, was of course Senator William H. Seward of New York. He was eminent in the legal profession. He had served with distinction as governor of his state before going to the Senate. He had been a leader of the antislavery Whigs and had brought them into the recently created Republican Party. He came to Chicago in the full expectation of being its nominee for President, and his supporters were ebulliently confident. But Seward carried the handicap of having been too long and too conspicuously the front-runner, so that he was the principal target of all the other candidates, and of this fact Judge David Davis, campaign manager for Abraham Lincoln of Illinois, took shrewd advantage. The bargaining for votes was ruthless, the argument that Seward's nomination would hopelessly alienate the South was pressed to the hilt, and the galleries of the Wigwam—the convention hall built for the occasion—were packed with leather-lunged Lincoln shouters brought in on counterfeit tickets while the Seward forces were parading through the streets on their optimistic way to the arena. When Lincoln's name was placed in nomination, reported an eyewitness, "five thousand people leaped to their seats, women not wanting, and the wild yell made vesper breathings of all that had preceded. A thousand steam whistles, ten acres of hotel gongs, a tribe of Comanches might have mingled in the scene unnoticed." Seward's lead on the first ballot was cut to a hair on the second, and on the third Lincoln was nominated. But behind and beneath their rivalry and contention Lincoln had

formed a true judgment of the quality of Seward, and one of his first acts after his election in November was to recruit Seward as Secretary of State.

Most of Lincoln's other Cabinet appointees were also closely connected with his search for the nomination. Some had, like Seward, been rival candidates. Others were holders of political due bills. Simon Cameron was one of these; he had delivered the Pennsylvania delegation for Lincoln. He wanted the Treasury portfolio; he got the War Department. Perhaps the only Cabinet officer not convinced he would have made a better President than Abraham Lincoln was Gideon Welles, the stubborn, tetchy, clear-headed Secretary of the Navy.

For the country the four months between election and inauguration were a strange, uneasy twilight. South Carolina seceded from the Union on December 20, and by the first of February six other states had followed suit. Northern sentiment was confused, and little leadership came from the White House, where old President Buchanan's policy seemed to be to close his eyes, block his ears, and pray for the speedy advent of Inauguration Day on March 4. Military posts in the seceding states were taken over or abandoned without struggle or even protest, and those that remained in Federal hands did so on the initiative of individual officers on the spot.

In South Carolina Major Robert Anderson found his position in Fort Moultrie untenable and moved to Fort Sumter in the middle of Charleston harbor. Even this withdrawal was branded by secessionists as a provocative gesture, and the ship that attempted to reprovision Sumter in early January was fired on and forced to withdraw.

In Florida on January 10—the very day that the state seceded—Union Lieutenant Adam J. Slemmer, in command of the two mainland forts at Pensacola, for like reasons withdrew his forty-odd men to Fort Pickens, situated on the western tip of Santa Rosa Island and commanding the entrance to the harbor. He was soon joined by some thirty sailors from the Pensacola Navy Yard. To reinforce this tiny garrison a contingent of soldiers was sent by sea. They didn't go ashore. Senator Stephen Mallory of Florida (soon to be secretary of the navy for the Confederacy) made an agreement with Buchanan, who had his own Secretaries of War and Navy issue orders that the Federal troops were not to land unless Fort Pickens was under actual or threatened attack. This so-called armistice of January 29 was still in effect, and troops under Captain Israel Vogdes were still aboard ship when Lincoln took office.

The new President's desires were not in doubt. He wished to preserve the Union; he did not wish war. He also said, in his inaugural address, "The power confided to me will be used to hold, occupy, and possess the property and places belonging to the Government." Seward had helped draft this speech. Yet within hours after the words were spoken, a message came in from Fort Sumter that without reprovisioning it could hold out no longer than forty days more. The President and his advisers were faced with the urgent need to examine and re-examine a quantity of choices, all unpleasant or dangerous.

Now as Seward brooded on these intricate and interlocking problems he became persuaded that the reinforcement of Pickens would demonstrate the firmness of the Federal will, without seeming so provocative as an attempt to resupply Sumter.

What Seward needed now was someone who could turn his policy into a concrete set of plans, someone qualified to determine what had to be done to reinforce that particular fort called Pickens at Pensacola in Florida —and to see that it was done. He must have blessed his stars when he realized that the ideal instrument was close at hand, that Captain Meigs could have been custom-tailored for the job.

Montgomery C. Meigs was an Army engineer. As a second lieutenant just out of West Point he had served for a year under Captain Robert E. Lee on a scheme to improve navigation in the Mississippi at St. Louis. Then came fifteen years of drudgery in the construction or refurbishing of inconsequential forts in various parts of the country. In November, 1852, Meigs had been assigned to survey the water supply for the cities of Washington and Georgetown, a survey for which Congress had just voted five thousand dollars. Three months later Meigs filed his report, offering three possible plans and strongly recommending the third: the building of an aqueduct from the Potomac just above Great Falls. His recommendation was accepted, and Congress forthwith appropriated a hundred thousand dollars to start construction. The new President, Franklin Pierce, assigned the task to the War Department, and the new Secretary of War, Jefferson Davis, put Meigs in charge of the works. (To this day Washington's water supply flows through the conduit that Meigs built. And that conduit is made of the same bricks that Meigs laid down in the 1850's.)

For good measure, Meigs was on the same day made disbursing agent and supervisory engineer for the extension of the Capitol and the modernization of both House and Senate chambers, a year-old project that had run into trouble. From the start Meigs— promoted within a month to first lieutenant and then to captain—was made responsible not to General Totten, the chief of engineers, but directly to the Secretary of War.

For four years this arrangement worked admirably. Relations between

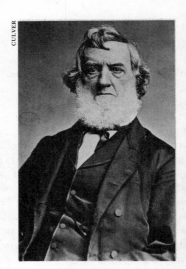

Gideon Welles

Winfield Scott

William H. Seward

Erasmus D. Keyes

Jefferson Davis and Meigs were harmonious, the Secretary gave the engineer great freedom of action, and work on both the aqueduct and the Capitol went forward speedily, efficiently, and without any hint of carelessness in the handling of public funds. In consequence Meigs was a familiar and respected figure on Capitol Hill.

In 1857, with the advent of the Buchanan administration, came a new and a demonstrated penchant for self-justification. So he and the Secretary were soon at daggers drawn, and their relationship grew steadily worse until, in November, 1859, an exasperated Floyd dismissed Meigs from the Capitol job. The captain turned to his friends in Congress, and an inquiry in the House concluded that Floyd's contracts for marble for the Capitol were illegal and that those made by Meigs should remain in force.

the lid they added a proviso that these funds could be expended only under the supervision of Captain Montgomery C. Meigs. As a practical matter President Buchanan could not veto the entire appropriation bill; he had to content himself with an opinion from the Attorney General that the proviso naming Meigs was not binding on the President, who as commander in chief had the constitutional right to reassign military officers. The contentious

Harper's Weekly, FEBRUARY 23, 1861

The stars and stripes gamely flying under a lowering sky, the imperiled Fort Pickens commands the waters of Pensacola Harbor, Florida.

Secretary of War, John B. Floyd of Virginia. Floyd had a considerably more relaxed attitude toward the public treasury than Meigs did. The captain was justly—and jealously—proud of his administration of the public works and determined to avoid any suspicion of graft in the letting of contracts or hiring of men. He also had a well-developed streak of self-righteousness and cantankerousness

Floyd's response came with the next War Department estimates, when he requested no money whatever for work on the aqueduct.

In no way daunted, Meigs went straight to the Senate, where Jefferson Davis was now chairman of the Military Affairs Committee. Davis and other admirers of Meigs wrote into the appropriation bill a half million dollars for the aqueduct. To nail down

letters that Meigs then addressed to the President as well as to Secretary Floyd ensured that a pretext would soon be found to put him out of the way. And, sure enough, in the autumn of 1860 Floyd removed Meigs from the waterworks and assigned him to construction at Fort Jefferson in the Dry Tortugas.

Meigs travelled overland to his new post, across the southern states. He was impressed by the scope and depth of secessionist sentiment and—when he reached his destination—by the sorry state of preparedness of the Florida forts.

Meigs devoted himself, with his usual vigor and efficiency, to improving the defenses of Fort Jefferson and also those of Fort Taylor at Key West. His sojourn in Florida was not long, however. By the end of December Secretary Floyd's record of slovenly management in the War Department had led to his forced resignation. On February 13 Meigs received orders to return to the aqueduct. He left the Dry Tortugas within two hours and on February 20 was in Washington, where he was promptly reassigned to the Capitol job as well.

So here, at Seward's elbow, was a trusted friend of long standing, an experienced engineer of proven competence, who knew from recent personal observation the plight of Fort Pickens and who had demonstrated beyond peradventure his willingness to proceed to an objective without undue regard for established channels of command.

Seward did not dawdle. Captain Meigs's diary for March 29 read thus:

To Great Falls. When we came home I found a request from the Secretary of State to come to see him. I went with him to the President who wished to see me. He said that they were in a difficulty and he wished to have the President talk with some man who would speak of what he knew—not of politics in military affairs and one who could get on a horse in the field too. He said they had had Gen. Scott and Gen. Totten but no one would think of putting either of these old men on horseback.

The President talked freely with me. I told him that men enough could be found to volunteer to endeavor to relieve Fort Sumter, but that persons of higher position and rank than myself thought it not to be attempted, that this was not the place to make the war, etc. He asked me whether Fort Pickens could be held. I told him certainly, if the Navy had done its duty and not lost it already. The President asked whether I could not go down there again and take a general command of these three great fortresses and keep them safe. I told him I was only a captain and could not command majors who were there. He must

take an officer of higher rank. Mr. Seward broke out with "I can understand too how that is, Captain Meigs, you have got to be promoted." I said "That cannot be done; I am a captain and there is no vacancy." But Mr. Seward told the President that if he wished to have this thing done the proper way was to put it into my charge and it would be done, that I would give him an estimate of the means by 4 P.M. of the next day. He complimented me much. Said that when Pitt wished to take Quebec he did not send for any old general but he sent for a young man whom he had noticed in the society of London, named Wolfe, and told him that he had selected him to take Quebec, to ask for the necessary means and do it and it was done. Would the President do this now? He replied that he would consider on it and would let me know in a day or two.

The seed was left to germinate in Lincoln's mind.

The third day, March 31, was Easter Sunday. Meigs has left an account of this day, but a fuller and livelier one comes from Lt. Colonel Erasmus D. Keyes, military secretary to General Winfield Scott. Keyes, who was serving his second tour of duty with the General, seems to have been a considerable talker, and at breakfast this morning he held forth for at least a half hour on the difficulties of landing artillery at Fort Pickens. When he had finished, General Scott handed him a map of Pensacola harbor, telling him to go straight to Secretary Seward and repeat this analysis. Let us listen to Keyes's account:

Arriving at Mr. Seward's house on F Street, I was admitted, and found the astute Secretary standing in the middle of his parlor alone. After a respectful salutation, I said:

"Mr. Seward, I am here by direction of General Scott, to explain to you the difficulties of reinforcing Fort Pickens."

"I don't care about the difficulties," said he. "Where's Captain Meigs?"

"I suppose he's at his house, sir."

"Please find him and bring him here."

"I'll call and bring him on my return from church."

"Never mind church today; I wish to see him and you here together without delay."

Notwithstanding I had been long subject to obey military commands implicitly, a rebellious thought arose in my mind, when I received from Secretary Seward such clear-cut orders. Nevertheless I reflected that he could speak from the am-

bush of original power, and concluded to obey him with alacrity, and within ten minutes Meigs and I stood together before him.

Without preliminary remarks, Mr. Seward said: "I wish you two gentlemen to make a plan to reinforce Fort Pickens, see General Scott, and bring your plan to the Executive Mansion at 3 o'clock this afternoon."

So off went Meigs and Keyes to the engineers' office, where they worked, almost without speaking to each other, for four hours. Then finding that the three o'clock deadline was upon them they went straight to the White House.

We found [this is Keyes speaking again] the President and the Secretary of State waiting to receive us. Mr. Lincoln was sitting behind the table near the end; his right leg, from the knee to foot, which was not small, rested on the table, his left leg on a chair, and his hands were clasped over his head. These positions were changed frequently during the conference, and I never saw a man who could scatter his limbs more than he.

At first Keyes was reluctant to read his contribution, pointing out that he and Meigs had not had time to show their work to Scott and that the General would be vexed at his secretary for by-passing him. So Meigs read his report, which concentrated on the engineering features of the operation. Keyes saw that though the two men had worked too rapidly to consult each other, his own report—dealing with the artillery aspects—meshed well with Meigs's. It may be this that emboldened him to give tongue. At any rate, he read out his recommendations. When he had finished, Lincoln told the two officers to go to Scott and tell him that the scheme had the President's approval and should proceed unless the general in chief saw strong reasons to the contrary. Then, according to Meigs, "We went to the house of General Scott, showed him our papers, which he approved saying there was nothing in them not necessary and little to be added as necessary. Mr. Seward came in and the matter was talked over and resolved upon."

But after Seward and Meigs had departed and the old general was left alone with his military secretary, the latter noted that his chief was struggling to restrain a tremendous emotion.

Next day, April 1, the scheme that had been approved in outline began to be translated into specific detail. Meigs and Keyes must have gone to work early with the various military bureaus in Washington to decide what units, what ordnance, what equipment should be assigned to the expedition. There was further discussion of whether Meigs could be put in command. This point was resolved when General Scott confirmed Meigs's own conclusion that it was impossible. So Colonel Harvey Brown was chosen as commander.

Later in the day a new character joined the action—Lieutenant David D. Porter of the Navy, brought into the picture by Meigs to handle the naval aspects of the enterprise. Porter's father, grandfather, and great-uncle had all been Navy officers. Porter's own career started when he accompanied his father on an expedition to suppress pirate forays in the West Indies. He was at the time ten years old. In the next few years he became a midshipman in the Mexican navy, and at sixteen he transferred to that of the United States. In late February or early March of 1861 he had received orders to take command of a coastal survey vessel on the Pacific Coast, and he was about to depart on this assignment. To continue in Porter's words:

My orders to California were still hanging over me, and I was taking my last meal with my family when a carriage drove up to the door.

It brought a note from the Secretary of State [Mr. Seward] requesting me to call and see him without delay; so, leaving my dinner unfinished, I jumped into the carriage and drove at once to the Secretary's office.

I found Mr. Seward lying on his back on a sofa, with his knees up, reading a lengthy document.

Without changing his position he said to me, "Can you tell me how we can save Fort Pickens from falling into the hands of the rebels?"

I answered promptly, "I can, sir."

According to Porter's account Meigs had approached him a few days earlier, and they had thrashed out a plan to "get a good-sized steamer and six or seven companies of soldiers, and to carry the latter, with a number of large guns and a quantity of munitions of war, to Fort Pickens, land them on the outside of the fort under the guns of a ship of war, and the fort would soon be made impregnable."

This then was the scheme that Porter outlined to Seward, adding, "Give me command of the *Powhatan*, now lying at New York ready for sea, and I will guarantee that everything shall be done without a mistake." At this point Meigs came in, and Seward, accompanied by his military and naval accomplices, went to the White House. There, in response to a question from Lincoln, Lieutenant Porter spoke:

"Mr. President" said I "there is a queer state of things existing in the Navy Department at this time. Mr. Welles is surrounded by officers and clerks, some of whom are disloyal at heart, and if the orders for this expedition should emanate from the Secretary of the Navy, and pass through all the department red tape, the news would be at once flashed over the wires, and Fort Pickens would be lost forever. But if you will issue all the orders from the Executive Mansion, and let me proceed to New York with them, I will guarantee their prompt execution to the letter."

"But," said the President, "is not this a most irregular mode of proceeding?"

"Certainly," I replied, "but the necessity of the case justifies it."

"You are commander-in-chief of the army and navy," said Mr. Seward to the President, "and this is a case where it is necessary to issue direct orders without passing them through intermediaries."

"But what will Uncle Gideon say?" inquired the President.

"Oh, I will make it all right with Mr. Welles," said the Secretary of State. "This is the only way, sir, the thing can be done. . . ."

It was finally agreed that my plan should be carried out. I wrote the necessary orders, which were copied by Captain Meigs and signed by the President, who merely said as he did so, "Seward, see that I don't burn my fingers."

Porter goes on to describe three of the orders that he had prepared. The first directed him to take command of the *Powhatan*, proceed to Fort Pickens,

and cover the fort while the reinforcements were landed. The second order instructed the commandant of the New York Navy Yard to fit out the *Powhatan* promptly and secretly and not to inform the Navy Department until the ship had sailed. The third order was directed to Captain Mercer, commander of the *Powhatan*. It detached him from the ship but assured him that this was no reflection on his competence and was done only because the ship's urgent and secret mission required a commander thoroughly conversant with the plan. But Porter makes no mention whatever of a fourth order, wholly unrelated to the mission, that he had prepared and slipped under the President's pen. This fourth order, since it had to do with the internal organization of the Navy Department, was promptly sent forward to the Secretary. It effectively torpedoed Secretary Seward's promise to "make it all right with Mr. Welles."

Its impact is best told in Uncle Gideon's own words:

On the 1st of April, while at my dinner at Willard's, where I then boarded, Mr. Nicolay, the private secretary of the President, brought to me and laid upon the table a large package from the President. It was between five and six o'clock in the afternoon when I received this package, which I immediately examined and found it contained several papers of a singular character, in the nature of instructions, or orders from the Executive in relation to naval matters, and one in reference to the government of the Navy Department more singular and remarkable than either of the others.

"This extraordinary document," as Welles calls it, was the fourth of the orders that Porter had just drafted. It relieved Captain Stringham from command of the Navy's Bureau of Detail, the office responsible for the assignment of all naval personnel, and replaced him by Captain Samuel Barron. Now Secretary Welles had come to rely greatly on Stringham, and he strongly suspected Barron of secessionist leanings.

Without a moment's delay [Welles says] I
CONTINUED ON PAGE 85

DON'T SPARE THE HORSES

*It's rough to be around a rider
when he's the President*

By CARY T. GRAYSON, JR.

ST. LOUIS *Republican*, JANUARY 15, 1909

In little more than seven weeks the Rough Rider would be leaving the White House. Nine months prior to his fifty-first birthday a still contagiously energetic Theodore Roosevelt was ready to demonstrate that his recent order setting physical standards for military promotion was not unreasonable. He believed that it was not too demanding to require Army and Navy officers either to walk fifty miles or to ride a hundred miles in three consecutive days.

So strong and so widespread had been the protests that the prescribed ride was a hardship upon the officers that the President was determined to find out for himself. Almost no one knew of the President's plan other than the White House physician, Admiral Presley M. Rixey, a Virginian who was Surgeon General of the Navy. Dr. Rixey did all he could to dissuade the President from what he feared would involve unnecessary risks. But even an appeal to Mrs. Roosevelt was useless, for she knew it would not do any good whatever for her to intervene.

There had been several good days of the best of winter weather when the President decided that on the next day, Wednesday, January 13, 1909, he, Admiral Rixey, and two younger White House aides, Army Captain Archibald "Archie" Butt of Georgia, and another Navy physician, Cary T. Grayson of Virginia, would ride to Warrenton, Virginia, and back in the course of the day—a distance estimated at more than ninety miles. Despite the weather bulletins predicting a blizzard for the next day the President left word that he be called at 2:30 A.M.

In the morning, after the President breakfasted on a considerable amount of rare steak and coffee, Admiral Rixey and the other members of the party arrived, and all underwent the brief physical examination that was part of the prescribed order for the riding test. Mr. Roosevelt submitted to it in good humor as the Admiral examined his heart and thumped him here and there. It was 3:40 A.M. when the four riders mounted their horses and, without delay, rode out of the White House gates. The ground was frozen hard, and there was a cutting cold wind blowing, but there was no sign of a blizzard in the sky. They started down Pennsylvania Avenue at a trot, the President on his horse Roswell, and after ten brisk minutes they crossed the bridge over the Potomac to Virginia.

The riding party skirted Fort Myer and made good time for the next six miles to Falls Church, but from there to Fairfax the roads were cut up and frozen with deep furrows that had not thawed in some time. After two and a half hours of hard riding from the White House they reached Fairfax, some twenty miles away, at 6:10 A.M. and in another ten minutes rode into Fairfax Court House, where a first change of horses was awaiting them.

The President had expected to see his favorite bay mare, Georgia, among the four waiting horses, which were attended by a trooper from the cavalry post at Fort Myer. Through some mix-up, however, the troopers, not knowing Mr. Roosevelt was in the party, had left Georgia behind. But the President showed no sign of anger and merely commented: "I am keenly disappointed, for I wanted Georgia to be in on this ride as a matter of sentiment if for nothing else." Actually he wanted no special favors and was determined that this ride be a test under just the conditions the average officer would be required to undergo. It was much harder, in fact, for the regular test rides were held only in the spring and fall and never in extreme heat or cold—and often with far better horses. The President had refused to let Captain Butt tell the commanding officer at Fort Myer why the horses were wanted and to what use they were going to be put. Since some of the horses were being sent to Admiral Rixey's nearby farm, it was believed that they were probably intended for a party of naval officers, and so naturally the Army had furnished less than their best animals.

The change to the new relay of horses took about ten minutes, and, starting at a good trot, the riders headed toward Centreville. Each rider probably had the same thought—that his new mount was about as disagreeable as could be turned out from a cavalry post. After forty-five minutes of riding they reached Centreville, halfway to Warrenton, and then, two miles farther on, came to a farmhouse

near Cub Run, where another change of horses was awaiting them. Unfortunately, this change was not for the better. The President's horse seemed even rougher and slower, and the one Captain Butt was riding showed a streak of viciousness toward the others. As a result there was not much conversation, but, as they passed the Bull Run battlefield, Mr. Roosevelt kidded Admiral Rixey and Dr. Grayson about the miserable state of their native Virginia roads. He also wondered what the spirits of the Federal troops would say if they saw him riding over Bull Run with "three rebels," as he called his three southern companions.

Although the plan had been to reach Warrenton by eleven o'clock, for some time the badly cut-up condition of the roads made it seem hopeless. Nevertheless, by the time they reached Gainesville, the riding party was gaining confidence that despite the difficult going the trip would be a success. Upon arriving at Buckland, less than ten miles from Warrenton, everyone seemed in fine humor as he changed horses for a third time and started on to Warrenton. As the riders became accustomed to their last relay of horses they kept off the side of the furrowed roads wherever possible, galloping whenever they could. Just as the town clock struck eleven, they entered Warrenton—seven hours and twenty minutes after their departure from the White House.

At this hour almost no one in Washington knew that the President had already ridden more than fifty miles and was now in Warrenton. It had been of little interest to anyone that a party of Navy officers apparently was going out on a day's jaunt, and relays of horses had been ordered for them from Fort Myer. Later the press was told that the chief executive had gone to Admiral Rixey's Virginia farm for a day's riding about the country, giving the President a midweek holiday of fresh air and exercise. There seemed to be no special news in that.

About six miles before the Presidential party reached Warrenton, a merchant in New Baltimore had recognized T.R. and after the riders had passed, had telephoned ahead to announce that the President of the United States was on horseback on his

way to Warrenton, where he would have lunch. A group of doubters in Warrenton went to the Warren Green Hotel, where they found several Secret Service men present and learned it was true that the President would have lunch there. Soon the cavalcade, headed by the President, appeared. Despite the cold, gray day a sizable crowd had gathered by the time the distinguished guest reached the old hotel. The grapevine news had spread quickly, and even the public schools had closed in honor of the Presidential visit.

At the Warren Green the President dismounted and made a short address to the assembled crowd of several hundred people, who gave him a rousing cheer. In a few moments Dr. John Wise, a retired Navy physician who was a personal friend of the Roosevelts and who now lived in Warrenton, joined Captain Butt in presenting the citizens of Warrenton to the President. A receiving line was formed just as it would have been at the White House, and Dr. Wise and Captain Butt presented each Warrentonian by name. For each, Mr. Roosevelt had some special words, but the result, unfortunately, was that the President had only about ten minutes in which to eat his lunch, as it was already nearly time to start back to Washington. He hurriedly drank two cups of tea and had some thick soup. Despite the chilly day and the hospitality offered them, no one in the riding party accepted anything in the way of alcoholic drink.

At 12:15 the riders were back in their saddles and soon were on their way, accompanied for a few miles by the master of the Warrenton Hunt and several other local riders. The ride back to Buckland, however, proved more difficult than the trip over the same terrain earlier in the day. Captain Butt was on a particularly fractious animal who "fought the bit the entire way...." Once when his rider dismounted to check the girth on the President's saddle, the horse reared and kicked, narrowly missing Dr. Grayson and his mount. The horse continued to rear and plunge, and it was fifteen minutes before the captain managed to get back on again. They did not reach Buckland until 1:35 P.M.

Here they changed to the same troop horses from Fort Myer that they had ridden to Buckland in the morning, but these animals seemed even worse than they had on their way out. Admiral Rixey led all the way back to Cub Run, but it was harder for the others who followed him to keep their horses at any kind of even pace. At Cub Run they changed horses for the next to last time, and the President ordered Captain Butt to set a good pace back to Fairfax. For some time they took advantage of the better stretches of road by galloping as long as possible; when they encountered poor road, they walked. On the whole the four men were somewhat exhilarated by their relatively good going and the knowledge that they were about halfway on their return journey to Washington. But just before Centreville the predicted storm struck, and a blizzard of blinding sleet descended from the north. As gale winds whipped and ice lacerated their faces the riders urged their horses at as fast a gait as possible, for it began to look doubtful that with darkness falling and increasingly heavy sleet they would be able to reach Washington.

When they arrived at Fairfax Court House, it was 5:10 P.M. Word by now was about that the President was on a hundred-mile ride, and despite the weather a small crowd had gathered to cheer him on. Here the riders remounted the horses that had begun the ride. Roswell, the President's trusted mount, was in good condition, and it was just as well, because from Centreville on, ice had begun to cake on Mr. Roosevelt's glasses so that he could hardly see where he was going. The President had expected to be back at the White House by seven o'clock, but now there was no such possibility, for twenty miles remained and the going was extremely bad.

From Fairfax the pitch darkness would have made for difficult riding in better weather, but with the sleet frozen on his glasses the President could see virtually nothing. He simply trusted Roswell to follow Captain Butt on the latter's faithful Larry. From Fairfax to Falls Church they had to walk practically the whole way. Once when they attempted to trot, the President's horse went into a ditch but luckily recovered without injury to himself or to his

rider. Dr. Grayson, who had been following behind the President, tried to lead the President's horse whenever he could, but he was having difficulties of his own, as his smooth-shod horse was slipping every few steps. The President warned him repeatedly to take no additional risks.

After Falls Church the roads were somewhat better, and although the sleet continued, the worst of the storm seemed to have passed. They were encouraged when they saw the reflected lights of Washington nine miles away. By now enough snow had fallen along with the sleet so that despite the difficulty caused by his glasses the President decided to try to make better time by trotting whenever possible. The footing proved far superior to what the horses had just been through, and they continued at a trot almost all the way to the Aqueduct Bridge over the Potomac. As the riders turned into the lighted approach to the bridge they could see a carriage from the White House waiting. Captain Butt had taken the precaution to send a telephone message from Fairfax to the White House to have them met because he did not believe it would be safe to ride across the bridge and then traverse the frozen streets to the White House. But the President brushed aside any thought of abandoning their horses short of the official terminus of the ride: "By George, we will make it to the White House with our horses if we have to lead them."

With the President in the forefront the riders crossed the bridge. The streets of Washington were "as slick as glass," and grass, shrubbery, and tree limbs glistened with clinging ice particles. The riders, followed by two mounted policemen and the empty carriage, made their way gingerly over ice-coated Pennsylvania Avenue. As they entered the grounds of the White House the four riders broke into a gallop. Mrs. Roosevelt was watching from a window. By the time they dismounted it was 8:40 P.M., and she was at the White House door to welcome them. All four were matted with snow and sleet, and the President was an especially striking figure in his broad-brim hat, black boots, and riding jacket

with fur collar, all fringed with ice. He admitted he was a little tired from being so much in the saddle and said he was sorry to be late for dinner. There was a brief physical examination, just as required of the military officers, and all were pronounced sound of wind and limb. Mrs. Roosevelt then gave each of them a julep, their first drop of liquor during the entire seventeen-hour ride. The President observed: "What has surprised me more than anything on this ride is the fact that no one has said a cross word, that we have had a good time, and that we returned laughing. . . . if we had not met this sleet storm, it would have been like taking candy from a child."

At his customary hour the next morning the President went to his office. Despite the ride the day before, which he now learned had been 104 miles, there was no sign that he had done anything unusual by way of physical exercise. The landscape for miles around Washington was covered with brittle ice particles that had fallen the previous afternoon and continued into the night. A newspaper headline proclaimed SLIPPERY DAY IN TOWN / SLEET STORM MAKES SKATING RINK OF CITY STREETS / MANY ARE HURT BY FALLS and went on to say that "old citizens described the conditions as the nastiest spell of weather Washington has been inflicted with for many years."

When queried by newsmen, the President said that the object of his long day in the saddle was "to prove to critics, who have found fault with the recent order requiring all army and navy officers to take a physical test, that if a President who is not in training, can ride 100 miles plus in one day without being laid up in bed thereby, it should not be too much to ask of men who are supposed to be in the best of physical training all the time to ride 100 miles in three days." The order would stand, and he expected that President Taft, when he came into office, would want to continue it. And, indeed, the policy was continued until World War I.

Cary T. Grayson, Jr., the publisher of Potomac Books, is a son of one of the participants in the 104-mile ride.

Veto

CONTINUED FROM PAGE 15

term were directed to private relief and pension bills. On one particularly busy day—March 4, 1895—he cast 57 pocket vetoes. Except for Franklin Roosevelt, Cleveland vetoed more bills than any other President, a grand total of 584 in eight years.

1944. **Franklin Roosevelt took to the veto power with a zest matched only by Cleveland. Old New Dealers tell the story that Roosevelt occasionally asked his aides for something he could veto in order to remind Congress not to get "uppity." True or not, the story underscores Roosevelt's record as "the vetoingest President" ever. By the time of his death in 1945 he had cast a total of 635 vetoes (372 regular, 263 pocket) and had been overridden only nine times.**

Roosevelt's vetoes ranged across public and private bills, pork-barrel construction projects, and what he took to be infringements of Presidential authority and, in a sense, reflect by themselves the history of the veto power. But one veto, in particular, is memorable both because it established a precedent and because the events surrounding it may have denied the Presidency to Alben W. Barkley, the majority leader of the Senate.

Early in 1944 Roosevelt had asked Congress for $10 billion in additional tax revenues to combat wartime inflation and hold down the national debt. When Congress passed a bill providing less than one billion, the famous Roosevelt temper flared, and he sent the bill back with a stinging veto message on February 22. This was the first time a revenue measure had been killed by a President, which by itself would have been a shock, but Roosevelt's words were more shocking still. "The bill," he wrote, "is replete with provisions that not only afford indefensible special privileges to favored groups, but set dangerous precedents." It is, he added, "a tax relief bill providing relief not for the needy but for the greedy."

Congress was stunned by the rebuke and then deeply angered. Barkley, in an impassioned speech that left him in tears, declared that the integrity of Congress had been wrongfully impugned, its members insulted, and the leadership demeaned. Immediately he announced his resignation as majority leader and withdrew. The next morning Roosevelt sent a telegram—instantly famous as the "Dear Alben" wire—in which he said he had no intention of attacking either the integrity of Congress or of its leadership. "You and I may differ . . . ," he said, "but that does not mean we question one another's good faith." He urged Barkley to return to the Senate and seek his leadership post. Barkley did and was unanimously re-elected majority leader. On February 25 Congress overrode Roosevelt's veto. Later in the year, when the time came for Roosevelt to choose a running mate for the coming election, he ignored Barkley, who until February had been the front-runner, and gave the nod to Senator Harry Truman of Missouri.

1947. Truman stands third on the list of Presidents who have cast the most vetoes. In seven years he exercised the veto 250 times (180 regular, 70 pocket). He was overridden twelve times, ranking him after Andrew Johnson

as the President most often overridden. Among the major pieces of legislation passed over his veto were the Taft-Hartley Act in 1947, the McCarran-Wood Internal Security Act of 1950, which required the registration of Communist Party members, and the McCarran-Walter Immigration and Naturalization Act of 1952, which established screening measures to keep out "subversive" aliens and empowered the Attorney General to deport naturalized Communists.

1964. **Lyndon Johnson, who vetoed 30 bills (16 regular vetoes, 14 pocket) may be the first President to have withdrawn a veto after he had earlier cast it. On August 24, 1964, he pocket-vetoed a bill that authorized the United States Court of Claims to hear a specifically identified suit against the government. Congress was in recess for the Democratic National Convention, and legally the bill was dead. Nonetheless two days later, and after Johnson had already drafted a message of disapproval to send to Congress, he changed his mind. He decided to sign the bill and leave the question of its constitutionality to the federal courts.**

1969–1973. Richard Nixon cast 39 vetoes through November, 1973 (22 regular, 17 pocket). He has been overridden five times. Like the majority of Presidents since Jackson—Lincoln is the one notable exception—he sees the veto as a weapon to shape public policy in accordance with his own political ideology. Lincoln, by contrast, shared Washington's view that the veto was a constitutional check and not an instrument of personal judgment. Virtually all Mr. Nixon's vetoes have been directed to spending measures and particularly to social programs of which he disapproves. Early in March, 1973, for example, he pledged that he would veto fifteen funding bills then before Congress and to date has vetoed four of them. The bills, said his chief aide, John Ehrlichman, were a "nine billion dollar dagger aimed at the heart of the American tax-payer." Were any of the bills to pass by override, Ehrlichman added, the President would impound the funds. This last statement is in line with the one significant addition Nixon has made to the veto power. Where earlier Presidents have accepted the override as binding, Nixon has thus far shown no disposition to do so. In the most controversial affair to develop to date he vetoed a water-pollution bill in October, 1972, but within hours the House overrode by a vote of 366–11 and the Senate by 74–0. Citing the "staggering costs" of the $24.6-billion measure over the next three years as justification, Nixon ignored the override and impounded the funds, which are currently the subject of court action.

Similarly, when Congress threatened a bill to cut off funding for the air war in Cambodia in the summer of 1973, Mr. Nixon announced that he would not pass the measure and would seek to get around it if he were overridden. A constitutional clash was avoided when the House sustained his veto and Nixon approved a compromise bill on July 1. Whether there will be other confrontations between Mr. Nixon and Congress on the veto power remains to be seen. ☆

The Making of an American Lion

CONTINUED FROM PAGE 11

tise that oiled an intricate commercial structure operating far from its base. Years afterward, when he became the first white man to navigate the length of the Congo River, he would draw on this American background, even discovering that the same sort of calico and sheeting that he had once handled on the Mississippi were being used as currency by the Kenya natives. On the Congo he would benefit from his memories of a flatboat trip he had made down the Mississippi and (in 1866) a similar voyage down the River Platte on a homemade raft.

Other tricks of the trade were also to be learned along the Mississippi and Arkansas rivers. Firstly, Stanley developed a phenomenal memory, which in later years was to stand him in such good stead as a newspaper reporter. Toward the end of his life his memory was so good that he could recall the precise names of casual acquaintances he had met as a teen-ager, and as a correspondent he was able to quote verbatim some conversations that he had heard five years before. River life also accustomed Stanley to constant travel, moving incessantly from one riverside market to the next and one plantation to another. Here, too, in the frontier atmosphere of Arkansas, where for a time he worked in a general store at Cypress Bend, he acquired an intimate knowledge of firearms, one of the main stock items, so that he could distinguish between a Sharp and a Ballard rifle or define the advantages of the Tranter over the Colt. Moreover, he learned to use these weapons. Cypress Bend had more than its fair share of feuds and larceny, and Stanley felt it necessary to practice with his gun behind the store until he became an accurate shot. Ironically, Cypress Bend also introduced him to another aspect of his future career, for it was there in the Arkansas bottom lands that Stanley first contracted ague, probably malaria, which reduced his weight to ninety-five pounds through repeated attacks of shivering, delirium, and nausea. With some truth he would one day point out to those who feared

the dangers of ill health for white colonists in East Africa that fever was more virulent and widespread along the lower Arkansas River.

The outbreak of the Civil War swept Stanley, somewhat reluctantly—he did not support the war or favor either side—into the Dixie Greys, a Confederate volunteer unit attached to the 6th Arkansas Regiment. On the second day of Shiloh he was taken prisoner by

Stanley at the age of fifteen in 1856, at about the time when he came to the United States. His name then was John Rowlands.

Union skirmishers and shipped north to Camp Douglas, a prison compound on the outskirts of Chicago. While conditions were not as bad as those at Andersonville, they were desperate enough to break all but the most hardy prisoners. Stanley was shocked. The inmates were emaciated, so many dying from dysentery and typhus that when Stanley saw the wagons call daily at the hospital he likened the corpses they collected, each wrapped in a blanket and piled one upon another, to "New Zealand frozen-mutton carcasses . . . carted from the docks!"

The Autobiography of Sir Henry Morton Stanley, 1909

After six weeks in the prison he volunteered to join the Northern forces and thereby obtained his release. Yet it was already too late. The young man—Stanley was only twenty-one years old—had scarcely been enrolled in the United States Artillery when he came down with a fierce attack of dysentery. As soon as he was fit enough to walk, the hospital authorities were only too glad to discharge him from their care and the Union forces, a physical wreck.

The next period of Stanley's life, from June, 1862, to the spring of 1867, was a mélange of half-baked ideas, half-finished projects, and misadventures. He went back to sea temporarily, survived a shipwreck off Spain, visited his mother in Wales but was rebuffed, and for the last eight months of the Civil War was enlisted as a clerk in the United States Navy. He saved enough money to launch an abortive expedition to Turkey, but he and his American companion were plundered by brigands and came home crestfallen, with financial aid from the American minister and consul general.

Yet there were two incidents in this period that had an important effect on Stanley. While in the Navy he was an eyewitness to the Federal attack at Fort Fisher, North Carolina, and wrote to newspapers describing the battle. Similarly, his dispatch recounting his misadventures in Turkey under the headline OUTRAGE TO AMERICAN TRAVELLERS IN TURKEY appeared in the press and attracted some attention. The result was that at the age of twenty-five Stanley decided to become a professional journalist, and, obtaining a roving commission from the editor of the Missouri *Democrat*, he set out in the spring of 1867, armed with note pad, pencil, and a valise of clothing, to report on the Army's campaigns to pacify the Cheyenne and Sioux Indians. Stanley's western tour was the last purely American lesson he learned, and in some ways it was the most important. His observations of the Indians, the workings of the negotiations between them and the military, the behavior of Generals Hancock and Sherman, who led the missions, and the exuberant development of the trans-Mississippi West that he wrote up, were all to shape his hopes for and ideas of Africa's peoples and prospects. He would paraphrase and quote to Congo natives speeches he had heard delivered to the Sioux; when attacked by Africans he reacted as if they were Indians on the warpath; and he dreamed of developing interior Africa in the same style he had seen in western America.

On his western travels, too, Stanley evolved his style of writing. His dispatches to the Missouri *Democrat* noticeably improved from the rather stilted early efforts to his more fluent descriptions of the cow towns and mining settlements that he visited toward the end of his journey. Stanley was never to become a really polished author, although he eventually wrote more than ten large volumes based on his travels. Instead, he could be relied upon to give a rambunctious, colorful account of his own escapades and impressions, written at phenomenal speed. And this was precisely what he gave the readers of the Missouri *Democrat,* whether telling them about the redoubtable chief Satanta of the Kiowa, who dressed in a captain's coat, with epaulets and leggings ornamented with jingling small brass bells, or describing Wild Bill Hickok, who was already a popular schoolboy hero. Hickok was working as a dispatch rider when Stanley met him, and evidently they struck up a friendship, for Stanley claimed that Hickok picked up a man who had insulted Stanley in a saloon and threw him over a billiard table.

Above all, Stanley's western dispatches brought him before the editors of larger city newspapers. Besides the Missouri *Democrat,* his reports appeared occasionally in papers in Chicago and New York, and it was in the latter city in 1868, after coming back from the West, that he asked James Gordon Bennett, Jr., for a job as an overseas correspondent for the *Herald.* Bennett gave him a trial posting as the correspondent to report on the British military campaign against Abyssinia, and Stanley succeeded bril-

liantly. On his way there he bribed the telegraph master at Suez to give priority to any dispatches for the *Herald,* transmitting them before any other traffic. Thus Stanley's descriptions of the British victory at Magdala were sent over the wires even before General Robert Napier's official announcement to the British government. By another stroke of Stanley's luck, the cable to England then broke, and for the next few days Her Majesty's government found itself obliged —to its intense annoyance—to learn about the country's great victory exclusively from the columns of the New York *Herald.*

The Abyssinian scoop confirmed Stanley as a crack correspondent and in due course led to the imperious summons to editor Bennett's presence for the great journalistic commission that would result in Livingstone's rescue. In typical Bennett style neither money nor time was to be any hindrance to his reporter's quest. As he

put it to Stanley: "Draw a thousand pounds now; and when you have gone through that, draw another thousand, and when that is spent, draw another, and when you have finished that, draw another thousand, and so on; but, FIND LIVINGSTONE."

Nearly everything about Stanley's expedition was markedly American. With the backing of an American newspaper Stanley arrived in Zanzibar on a Yankee ship on January 6, 1871, and went promptly to seek the help of the American consul there, deliberately taking care to keep his real intentions hidden from the British diplomatic representative. The American community of Zanzibar could not have been more helpful. Because there was no money waiting for Stanley from Bennett, the consul, Captain Francis R. Webb, advanced Stanley money to buy stores. Webb's wife herself stitched together the American flag that was to be borne, Stanley ordered, by the tallest Negro in his column. And the small

Unlike his aborted lecture series in 1872, Stanley's lecture tour in 1890 and 1891 was an immense success. Together with his wife—shown here standing beside him—he travelled across the United States in a special Pullman car named in his honor. She called it palatial.

In 1885, when this photo was taken, Stanley applied for American citizenship to protect the copyright on his books published here.
The Autobiography of Sir Henry Morton Stanley, 1909

American mercantile community at Zanzibar, mostly New Englanders (Salem had a long tradition of trade with Zanzibar), helped him to assemble his stores and even presented him with a horse on which to lead his expedition.

By the same token, the chagrin of the English when Stanley reappeared out of central Africa to announce his success was immediate. "It is with some regret," declared the reporter for the London *Daily Telegraph*, "that I must commence by saying that Mr. Stanley is not an Englishman, or rather a Welshman, as was recently reported in some journals, but an American citizen." Other newspapers complained about having to learn about Livingstone through the columns of the New York *Herald*, and several critics—including some American newspaper rivals—claimed that Stanley was a fraud and had never actually met Livingstone. On the whole, however, Americans were delighted with Stanley's success, and in particular he be-

came a symbol for the expatriate Americans living in Europe. In Paris, for example, the American community led by Minister Washburn organized a dinner at the Hotel Chatham to which Stanley was invited on his way back from Africa. Another guest was William Tecumseh Sherman, then touring Europe and the Middle East, and Stanley took huge delight in quoting from memory to the general the speech Sherman had made to the Indians when Stanley was a reporter with his command.

Stanley initially repaid his transatlantic compliments by burying his Welsh background and playing up his American antecedents. It was a deliberate ruse, because someone in England had dug up Stanley's Welsh birthplace and Stanley flatly denied the fact. For whatever reason—reluctance to admit his humble birth, gratitude to America for his training, or as an American by choice—Stanley emphasized his American background and did not correct the statements that variously described his birthplace as Ohio, Illinois, Missouri, and New York.

Naturally the deception could not be maintained forever, and in the long run this served Stanley's purpose just as well. Africa, after all, was of much greater interest to imperial Britain than to the United States, and as Stanley's African career developed he received more sympathy and cooperation from the British. It was a gradual process of readjustment by which he managed to retain both his American and his British links. His Congo voyage, for example, was sponsored jointly by the New York *Herald* and the London *Daily Telegraph* and flew both the American and the British flags; and though at the end of the journey Stanley advocated that Britain should claim the Congo for herself, he appeared at the Berlin Conference, which decided such matters, as an adviser to the American delegation. Indeed in 1885, so as to protect the copyright of his books in the United States, he formally became an American citizen before the superior court of New York City.

But chiefly he was thought of in an African context. He was held to be the African traveler par excellence, the

man who would succeed where all others might fail. Thus in 1887, when a relief expedition was raised to send to the help of Emin Pasha, the governor of Equatorial Province cut off by rebels in the Sudan, it was Stanley who was picked to lead the armed flying column. Once again by a combination of ruthless discipline and single-minded efficiency Stanley thrust his way across Africa. Emin Pasha was escorted out, and Stanley came back to Europe an international hero. Now everyone was falling over themselves to pay him honors. Belgium gave him a state reception, and its king awarded him the Grand Cross of the Order of Leopold and the Grand Cross of the Congo. In London the Royal Geographical Society struck a special gold medal for him—it was his second, an honor never before or since accorded —and organized a huge meeting in Albert Hall attended by the Prince of Wales. The American community in London put on a sumptuous testimonial dinner, embellishing the occasion with menu books bound in hand-tooled leather (which several guests filched) and gave to Stanley a special two-foot-high silver and gold shield ordered from Tiffany's, which depicted Africa beneath an American eagle. In Iceland a local poet composed an ode to Stanley, loosely derived from *Hiawatha*, and Stanley's book of the expedition, *In Darkest Africa*, was so widely successful that it helped establish that phrase as a popular catchword in much the same way as his earlier remark, "Dr. Livingstone, I presume."

This spate of acclaim signified the high-water mark of Stanley's career. The price of his success had been the ruin of his health, which now forced his virtual retirement from active exploration. In 1890 at Westminster Abbey he married Dorothy Tennant, the daughter of a wealthy landowner, but he was so wracked with illness that a physician had to accompany the couple on their honeymoon. Thereafter his spells of gastritis, as he called them, became increasingly debilitating. His wife, too, served as a restraining influence. Partly at her suggestion Stanley entered British politics, applying to the home secretary for readmission to British citizenship so that he could run for Parliament, though as an M.P. Stanley made little impact and soon gave up the position. However, his new nationality did mean that the royal office could at last recognize his achievements, and on May 19, 1899, he was sent a letter informing him that "Her Majesty has been pleased to confer upon you the Grand Cross of the Bath." The erstwhile Welsh runaway was finally Sir Henry Morton Stanley.

At no time, however, did he forget those early days in America that first launched him on his phenomenally successful life. In 1890, as the most successful African explorer of his day and the friend of kings, prime ministers, and millionaires, he came back to America to make a lengthy lecture tour. This time it was a great success.

He travelled from one end of the country to the other in a special private Pullman car named the Henry M. Stanley, complete with its own kitchen and cook, a dining section that converted at night into a dormitory, a drawing room with a piano, three state bedrooms, and a bathroom.

The tour was also a pilgrimage for Stanley. Everywhere he went, he looked again for the places that he remembered from his youth. He paid a visit to New Orleans, strolled nostalgically up Tchapitoulas Street, and took his aristocratic English wife to the French market to treat her to what he claimed was a "cup of the best coffee in the world" from Monsieur Morel's coffee stand there. Stanley also examined the Civil War battlefields and called at some of the towns he had originally described in the Missouri Democrat.

Stanley remained a fervent romantic about America. After his death, when the time came to make an inventory of the great explorer's belongings, the researchers found boxes and trunks neatly labelled and organized in a manner typical of his tidy mind. In one trunk they found a small collection of Civil War mementos, including several Confederate notes, eagle buttons, three belt clasps, and eleven minié balls. But most extraordinary of all, among the heaps of African shields and spears, the Pygmy poisoned arrows, and all the paraphernalia of his great African trips on which he had found tribes previously unknown to the white man, Stanley had carefully preserved a broken stone peace pipe of the sort so commonly found in the American West. According to its label, it was believed to have once belonged to Chief Sitting Bull.

Timothy Severin is an English writer who specializes in the history of exploration. He is the author of The Horizon Book of Vanishing Primitive Man, *which was published last year by this company, and is currently at work on a book about travellers and explorers in the Far East.*

The Relief of Fort Pickens

CONTINUED FROM PAGE 77

went to the President with the package in my hand. He was alone in his office and, raising his head from the table at which he was working, inquired, "What have I done wrong?" I informed him I had received with surprise the package containing his instructions respecting the Navy and the Navy Department, and I desired some explanation. I then called his attention particularly to the foregoing document, which I read to him. This letter was in the handwriting of Captain Meigs of the army, the postscript in that of David D. Porter.

The President expressed as much surprise, as I felt, that he had sent me such a document. He said Mr. Seward with two or three young men, had been there through the day on a subject which he (Seward) had in hand, and which he had been some time maturing; that it was Seward's specialty to which he, the President, had yielded, but as it involved considerable details, he had left Mr. Seward to prepare the necessary papers. These papers he had signed without reading—for he had not time, and if he could not trust the Secretary of State, he knew not whom he could trust. I asked who were associated with Mr. Seward. "No one," said the President, "but these young men

were here as clerks to write down his plans and orders." Most of the work was done, he said, in the other room. I then asked if he knew the young man. He said one was Captain Meigs, another was a naval officer named Porter. . . .

He gave me at that time no information of the scheme which Mr. Seward had promoted, further than that it was a specialty which Mr. Seward wished should be kept secret. I therefore pressed for no further disclosures.

But the President did tell Welles that he could disregard the order naming Barron to replace Stringham in charge of United States Navy personnel. And just as well. It soon came to light that Barron had already accepted a commission in the Confederate navy. (It is still a mystery why Porter attempted to get Barron put in charge of the United States Navy Bureau of Detail. Porter's own narrative never mentions the incident. Welles believed that Porter himself was wavering between the Union and the Confederacy and that it

was his participation in the Pickens expedition that brought him down on the Union side.)

At some point in this eventful day the President also received from his bumptious Secretary of State a startling memorandum. It was another and more explicit revelation of Seward's view that he should, in effect, serve as prime minister of the administration over which Lincoln presided. It began in forthright, if somewhat insubordinate, fashion: "We are at the end of a month's administration and yet without a policy either domestic or foreign." In the domestic field Seward wished, he told Lincoln, to "change the question before the public from one upon slavery, or about slavery, for a question of union or disunion." As a further means of fostering domestic solidarity Seward proposed that the United States should adopt a truculent attitude toward Spain, France, Great Britain, and Russia and suggested that if the two former countries failed to give what he referred to as "satisfactory explanations" of certain recent actions in Mexico and Santo Domingo, Congress should be convened to declare war against them. "But whatever policy we adopt," wrote Seward, "there must be an energetic prosecution of it. . . . Either the President must do it himself . . . or devolve it on some member of his Cabinet. . . . It is not in my especial province; but I neither seek to evade nor assume responsibility." This offer to take over the duties of the Presidency was politely but very firmly rejected, on the same day and in writing, by Abraham Lincoln.

Now Meigs, Keyes, and Porter moved their base of operations to New York. Meigs had ten thousand dollars in coin that Seward had given him from secret State Department funds. (When the expedition was over, Meigs turned back six thousand dollars of this advance.) He and Keyes busied themselves with assembling men, horses, and guns and in chartering steamers to carry them to Florida. Porter concentrated on making good his claim to command of the *Powhatan*, and a troublesome task it proved to be. To his great satisfaction he found that the commandant of the Navy Yard was on leave. This officer had a reputation for caution and would probably have insisted on telegraphing the Navy Department for confirmation of Porter's orders.

As it was [this is Porter's account], I had trouble enough with Foote [the acting commandant] to bring him to reason, and it was only after three hours earnest conversation that I convinced him I was not a rebel in disguise plotting with the Powhatan's officers to run away with the ship, and deliver her over to the South.

"You see, Porter," he said, "there are so many fellows whom I would have trusted to the death who have deserted the flag that I don't know whom to believe." He read my orders over and over, turned them upside down, examined the water-mark and Executive Mansion stamp, and surveyed me from head to foot. "How do I know you are not a traitor? Who ever heard of such orders as these emanating direct from the President? I must telegraph to Mr. Welles before I do anything, and ask further instructions."

"Look at those orders again," I said, "and

then telegraph at your peril. . . . If you must telegraph, send a message to the President or Mr. Seward."

"Yes," replied Foote, "and what would prevent you from having a confederate at the other end of the line to receive the message and answer it—there is so much treason going on?"

I burst out laughing. "What would you say," I inquired, "if I were to tell you that [Navy Captains] Frank Buchanan, Sam Barron, and [George] Magruder were going to desert to the rebels?"

Foote jumped from his chair. "God in heaven!" he exclaimed, "what next? You don't expect me to trust you after that? . . . But, man, that can't be, for I saw by the morning papers that President Lincoln was at a wedding last night at Buchanan's, and Buchanan had the house festooned with American flags, and all the loyal men of

Federal reinforcements file ashore under the guns of the fort on the morning of April 13.
Harper's Weekly, MAY 18, 1861

Washington were there."

"So they were," I replied, "but, nevertheless, they will all desert in a few days, for their hearts are on the other side. [Captain Duncan] Ingraham is going also—his chief clerk has already preceded him, and carried off the signal book of the navy."

"Good Lord deliver us!" exclaimed Foote, piously. "I must telegraph to Mr. Welles. I can't stand this strain any longer. It will kill me. You sit smoking and smiling as if this was not a very serious matter." "Here"—to his chief clerk—"bring me a telegraph blank."

Porter's debonair account of this interview is too long to give in full. But one more passage is worth repeating.

"Just think," I continued to Captain Foote, "of the President taking you into his confidence so early in these troubles; think what a high position you may reach before the trouble with the South is over if we succeed in carrying out this expedition successfully. Then, again, think what a tumble you will get if you disobey a positive order of the President. He will believe rebellion rampant everywhere, and won't know whom to trust. Think of Captain Foote being tried and shot like Admiral Byng for failing to carry out his orders."

The unhappy Foote succumbed to these persuasions, but he took Porter to stay at his own house, where he could be observed and, if things went wrong, apprehended.

Meanwhile, back in Washington, preparations for the relief of Fort Sumter were in full swing. The War Department had general responsibility, but naval vessels were of course needed to support the expedition. On April 5 Secretary Welles prepared orders and read them to the President, and upon his approval they were promptly dispatched. They were addressed to Captain Samuel Mercer, commanding United States steamer *Powhatan*, and instructed him to take three additional ships under his command and proceed to Charleston.

The impact of this message in New York is not hard to imagine. Excerpts from Meigs's diary give the story succinctly and poignantly.

April 5 ... Evening, telegram from Secretary of Navy to detain the *Powhatan*. Porter in despair. Says he will do nothing more for this government. He will go to California and spend his time in surveying. ...

April 6. Everywhere. Had to go to the Navy Yard to endeavor to save the *Powhatan*. This did twice, and I succeeded in taking her though written orders from Secretary of Navy to send her to help reinforce Sumter on the 11th were in the yard. I took the ground that Capt. Mercer had been relieved by orders signed by President, that she was promised to our expedition, was a necessary and most important part of it, and that no man, secretary or other, had a right to take her, and that the secretary could not do it as I was by the President made responsible and told not to let even the Secretary of the Navy know that this expedition was going on. They gave her up to us and Porter sailed about noon. He was seen going down the harbor at 3 P.M.

But Porter wasn't yet home free. For some unexplained reason Meigs couldn't let well enough alone. Obviously he must have been bone weary and nervously exhausted from the varied physical and emotional stresses of the past few days. At any rate, perhaps in an uncontrollable welling up of his own persnickety brand of self-righteousness, Meigs shot off a wire to Seward, complaining of the interference of the Secretary of the Navy. On receiving Meigs's message Seward also lost sight of the salutary maxim that you should quit when you're ahead. Secretary Welles describes the consequences:

I congratulated myself, when I went to my room at Willard's on the evening of the 6th of April, that [the preparation of the Sumter expedition] had been accomplished within the time given us, and that the force had probably sailed.
Between eleven and twelve that night, Mr. Seward and his son Frederick came to my rooms at Willard's with a telegram from

Captain Meigs at New York, stating in effect that the movements were retarded and embarrassed by conflicting orders from the Secretary of the Navy. I asked for an explanation, for I could not understand the nature of the telegram or its object. Mr. Seward said he supposed it related to the *Powhatan* and Porter's command. I assured him he was mistaken, that Porter had no command, and that the *Powhatan* was the flagship, as he was aware, of the Sumter expedition. He thought there must be some mistake, and after a few moments' conversation, with some excitement on my part, it was suggested that we had better call on the President. Before doing this, I sent for Commodore Stringham, who was boarding at Willard's and had retired for the night. When he came, my statement was confirmed by him, and he went with us, as did Mr. Frederick Seward, to the President. On our way thither Mr. Seward remarked that, old as he was, he had learned a lesson from this affair, and that was, he had better attend to his own business and confine his labors to his own Department. To this I cordially assented.

One can have some doubt whether Mr. Seward's contrition was as clearly expressed as Mr. Welles tells us. It was certainly not in evidence when the group came before the President. Seward argued tenaciously that the *Powhatan* should remain committed to the relief of Fort Pickens. The President himself found it hard to believe that the *Powhatan* had indeed been assigned to the Sumter expedition. But when Welles went to the Navy Department and returned with copies of the orders, the President was convinced. He instructed Seward to send a telegram ordering that the *Powhatan* be at once restored to Captain Mercer. Seward protested, but, says Welles,

The President would not discuss the subject but was peremptory, ... and he directed Mr. Seward to telegraph ... to New York without ... delay. Mr. Seward thought it might be difficult to get a telegram through, it was so late, but the President was imperative.

Fortunately we have no witness to the state of Captain Foote's emotions when, hours after Porter and the *Powhatan* had disappeared down the bay, this new order was received at the Navy Yard. But he was prompt to send it forward by a fast tug, and the *Pow-*

hatan was in fact overtaken before she got to Staten Island. The message was clear enough; it read "Deliver up the *Powhatan* at once to Captain Mercer." The signature at the end was clear also; it was "Seward," not "Lincoln."

This was a loophole with which Porter was intimately familiar, and he was through it in the twinkling of an eye.

I telegraphed back [says he], "Have received confidential orders from the President, and shall obey them. D. D. Porter"
I then went on deck and gave orders to go ahead fast. In an hour and a half we were over the bar, discharged the pilot, and steering south for an hour, and then due east, to throw any pursuers off our track (for I was determined to go to Fort Pickens). At sundown I steered my course.

Let us turn now to the situation at Fort Pickens itself, where the relief force under Captain Vogdes was still confined aboard ship in compliance with the instructions of the Buchanan administration. On March 12 General Scott had sent orders for the soldiers to land, but no response had been received in Washington. Then on April 6 a message came to Secretary Welles from Captain Adams, the officer commanding the naval force off Fort Pickens. Scott's orders, sent by sea, had not been received until April 1. Adams, feeling himself still bound by the Navy Department's instruction of January 30 and not subject to the orders of General Scott, an Army officer, had refused to let Captain Vogdes land his troops. Adams' message asked urgently for direction from the new administration's Secretary of the Navy. Off went Welles to the White House, where it was soon agreed, first, that the troops should be landed and, second, that the telegraph was too insecure a way to transmit the required orders. So another messenger, Lieutenant John Lorimer Worden, was briefed, told to memorize and destroy his orders, and sent off overland. He reached Pensacola on the morning of April 11 and requested permission to communicate with the United States fleet. This was a privilege expressly granted by the January 29 armistice, and that afternoon Worden was aboard the dispatch boat. But there was too much sea to cross the bar that night, and it was not until noon on April 12 that he delivered his message to Captain Adams.

At about the same hour General Braxton Bragg, commanding the Confederate forces at Pensacola, received from his war department this telegram: "Lt. Worden of US Navy has gone to Pensacola with dispatches. Intercept them." The unfortunate Bragg had to reply that Worden had come and gone, that alarm guns had just been fired at Fort Pickens, and that reinforcements would probably be landed before morning. He was correct; Captain Vogdes' men, along with a hundred fifteen marines, went ashore that night.

On April 16 the expeditionary force of Colonel Brown and Captain Meigs arrived at Fort Pickens, approaching the island on the seaward side and offloading without incident two hundred soldiers that night and the rest of the men and cargo, including the horses, on the seventeenth. Also on the seventeenth the *Powhatan*, whose mission had been to cover the landing, hove somewhat anticlimactically into view.

Her commander, though coming late to the feast, did his best to bring drama to the occasion. He appeared flying the British flag, apparently hoping to run past the shore batteries and enter the harbor itself. The businesslike Colonel Brown did not relish the idea of having his landing parties harassed by the Confederate fire that Porter seemed intent on provoking. So Meigs was dispatched on an errand that, in a final flourish of bravado, Porter reports thus:

I ran in for the harbor, crossed the bar, and was standing up to Round Fort, when a tug put out from Pickens and placed herself across my path. Captain Meigs was on board the tug, waving a document, and, hailing, said he had an order from Colonel Brown. It was to the following effect: "Don't permit *Powhatan* to run the batteries or attempt to go inside. It will bring the fire of the enemy on the fort before we are prepared."
I felt like running over Meig's tug, but obeyed the order. The stars and stripes were hoisted, in hopes the enemy would open fire, but they did not, nor do I believe they had any intention of so doing.

The relief of Fort Pickens had been accomplished.

The aftermath is tame enough. Pickens remained in Union hands throughout the war, and the Confederacy was deprived of the harbor of Pensacola. Indeed the Confederate forces eventually destroyed the dry dock at the Navy Yard and evacuated the town of Pensacola itself, which was forthwith occupied by the Federals.

It is more interesting to take a brief look at the later history of some of the participants in the Pickens venture. Captain Meigs, you recall, had been barred from command of the expedition because of his rank and because no vacancy existed for his promotion. But in the spring of 1861 the times they were a'changing—and fast. From Fort Pickens, Meigs returned to Washington, where on May 14 he was made colonel and on May 15 was appointed brigadier general and quartermaster general of the Union Army, to succeed Colonel Joseph E. Johnston, who had gone south to the Confederates. As quartermaster general throughout the war, Meigs enhanced his reputation for integrity and efficiency, and he held the post for twenty years.

Porter continued in his headstrong and flamboyant way. Luckily for him and for his cause, his abilities outweighed his indiscretions, and his services in the Gulf, at New Orleans, and at Vicksburg won him promotion to rear admiral. After the war he was a notable superintendent of the Naval Academy, and when the rank of admiral fell vacant with the death of his foster brother David Farragut, Porter succeeded him—the second of that rank in the history of the United States Navy.

Lieutenant Colonel Keyes was delayed in his return from New York. Secessionists had torn up the railroad and destroyed bridges around Baltimore, and Keyes came back by way of Annapolis, in the company of the 7th New York Regiment. He found that an exasperated General Scott had taken another military secretary in his stead. Be it remembered not only that Keyes had absented himself overlong

on this extracurricular frolic with Meigs and Porter, but also that he had got into it in the first place when he had been sent by his chief to explain to Secretary Seward why the Pickens expedition should *not* be undertaken.

However, by the end of May, Keyes had a commission as brigadier general of volunteers, in which capacity he earned a commendation at the First Battle of Bull Run. In the Peninsular Campaign he commanded one of McClellan's corps. Later a dispute with General John Adams Dix led to his resignation from the Army.

Lieutenant Worden, the officer who had slipped through Bragg's fingers at Pensacola to deliver the message that sent Vogdes' men ashore, made the mistake of trying to return north overland instead of by sea. This time his luck failed him, and he spent seven months in a Confederate prison. He was exchanged just in time to take command of the *Monitor* in her fight with the *Merrimack*. After the war he succeeded Porter as superintendent of the Naval Academy.

Captain Foote, from whose custody Meigs and Porter had pilfered the *Powhatan*, was in August, 1861, placed in command of naval operations on the upper Mississippi. Early the next year the heavy attack of his flotilla against Fort Henry compelled that strong point to surrender even before the arrival of Grant's army forces. Foote distinguished himself also at Island No. 10 in the Mississippi and was promoted to rear admiral but died before the end of the war.

Seward continued to lord it over Welles, and Welles continued to snap at Seward. But both men served Lincoln well and loyally to the end. They were the only two of his original Cabinet officers to stay on throughout Andrew Johnson's administration, and both of them were notable for the wholehearted support they gave to that beleaguered President when the venomous radicals of the Senate attempted, through an impeachment trial, to remove him from office.

James Cooley, a retired lawyer, has spent most of his career in government service. This is his first magazine article.

The Arts of Diplomacy

CONTINUED FROM PAGE 31

now presented to the United States.... [They] will be deposited with the archives of the United States, which are at once the evidence and the memorials of their freedom and independence.

The first two Presidents surrounded themselves with a certain amount of pomp and ceremony as a means of demanding respect for the new office of the Presidency. But when Thomas Jefferson was inaugurated, all protocol went by the board, and the atmosphere in the White House became so studiedly informal that some representatives of foreign governments were insulted. Jefferson for his part did not hide his disapproval when the French minister, Gerneral Louis Marie Turreau de Garambouville, Baron de Linières, presented his credentials in 1804 in clothing heavily ornamented with gold lace. The President later remarked to John Quincy Adams that "they must get him [Turreau] down to a plain frock coat, or the boys in the streets will run after him as a sight."

Jefferson was also scrupulous about receiving gifts. Even from American citizens he said he would not accept anything but a pamphlet, a book, or some curiosity of small enough value to be "below suspicion." Many Presidents deemed it proper for their wives or children to accept presents, since they do not hold "any office of profit or trust," but Jefferson would not permit his daughter to keep a cashmere shawl presented by the ambassador from Tunis. Although it was accepted ceremoniously as an expression of the good will of the bey of Tunis, it was sold at auction, and the proceeds were deposited in the Treasury.

Through the years the enforcement of Article I, Section 9 produced several tragicomic incidents. In 1839 Thomas N. Carr, United States consul at Tangier, was forced to accept a dismaying present. The story is best told in the words of his report to the Secretary of State:

Sir,

I am sorry to inform the Department that, although I have exerted myself to the utmost to prevent the presentation of any animals from the Emperor [of Morocco], and to convince his ministers of the impossibility of accepting a gift or present of any kind, my exertions have not been attended with success....

[Having failed to convince the Emperor's officers of my earnestness], I resolved to write to the Emperor himself, but before a letter could be prepared the sound of drums announced the arrival of the Bashaw's Nephew at the head of a troop of soldiers with an enormous, magnificent *Lion & Lioness.*

As my determination was well known, the commander of the troop had prepared himself with the most "conclusive answers" to all my objections. I told him that [it] was perfectly impossible to receive the animals, the Laws of my Country forbid it. He replied that they were not for me, that they were for my Government. I told him that the President, the head of my Government, was in the same predicament as myself, that he had not the power to receive them. He said that the Sultan knew that but that they were not for the President but for my Congress. I replied that Congress had resolved never to receive any more presents, and that the Law prohibiting Public Officers to receive presents was part of the Constitution, & superior to the power of Congress itself. He wanted to know who made the Constitution, I replied the people [;] then said he if Congress will not receive them the Emperor desires them to be presented to the people, as a mark of his respect and esteem for the "Sultans" of America.

At last I told him that *I would not receive them,* that my mind was fully made up; then said he, my determination is as strong as yours; I am ordered to deliver them to you; it will cost me my head if I disobey; I shall leave them in the street.

The street upon which is the American Consulate is a narrow *Cul de sac* with a half dozen few houses in it beside my own. Preparations were made for placing a guard at the open end, and turning the lions loose in the street. Seeing further resistance hopeless ... I was compelled to surrender to this novel form of attack, and to open one of my rooms for the reception of the animals where they now are....

I hope that I shall have the honour, and pleasure, of hearing upon this subject from the Department as soon as possible.

At virtually the same time, the imam of Muscat dispatched to President Martin Van Buren a magnificent selection of gifts including two Arabian horses, a bottle of attar of roses, five demijohns of rosewater, a package of cashmere shawls, a bale of Persian rugs, and a box of pearls. The consent of Congress to receive all this bounty was requested, and a resolution authorizing the acceptance and sale of the Moroccan lions and the gifts from Muscat was reported out of the House Committee on Foreign Relations by its chairman, future President James Buchanan. It was passed, but only over the bitter protest of former President John Quincy Adams, then representing Massachusetts in the lower house. In his journal he wrote: "I ... affirmed that Congress never had in any one instance authorized the acceptance of presents." Two days later he was still agitated about the matter: "No small part of this day," he wrote, "was engaged in hunting up documents respecting the acceptance of presents by officers of the United States from foreign powers."

The Moroccan lions were shipped to Philadelphia on the brig *Tacon* at a cost to the United States government of six hundred fifty dollars. They disappeared from the scene when they were sold at auction in the Philadelphia Navy Yard on August 31, 1840, to a Mr. Robert Davis for $375.

An interesting exchange took place between President Abraham Lincoln and His Majesty Somdetch Phra Paramendr Maha Mongut, King of Siam. Lincoln's predecessor, James Buchanan, had sent the king a present of government publications to indicate his pleasure in the ratification of a commercial treaty with Siam in 1856. The king responded by sending a handsome sword in a gold scabbard inlaid with silver, a daguerreotype portrait of himself and his child, and a pair of elephant tusks. He took into account both the length of the voyage between Bangkok and Washington and the American custom of rotation in office when he addressed his accompanying letter to

> His Most Respected Excellent Presidency, The President of United States of America, who having been chosen by the Citizens of the United States as most distinguished, was made President and Chief Magistrate in the affairs of the Nation for an appointed time of office.

In addition to thanking Buchanan, or "whomsoever the people have elected anew," the king declared that he had been informed that the United States had no elephants. He offered to remedy this deficiency, explaining that "elephants being animals of great size and strength [they] can bear burdens through uncleared woods and matted jungles where no carriage and cart roads have yet been made." He proposed to send several pairs that could be "turned loose in forests . . . [where] they will increase to be large herds. . . ." He gave detailed instructions in the care and feeding of elephants, saying that

> if the president of the United States and Congress who conjointly with him rule the country see fit to approve let them provide a large vessel loaded with hay and other food suitable for elephants on the voyage, with tanks holding a sufficiency of fresh water, and arranged with stalls so that the elephants can both stand & lie down in the ship—and send it to receive them. . . .
>
> When they arrive in America . . . let them with all haste be turned out to run wild in some jungle suitable for them. . . .

When the letter and presents arrived in the United States, Lincoln was President. If the handsome sword, the daguerreotype, and the king's letter in Siamese and English were superb examples of the arts of diplomacy, so were the words chosen by Abraham Lincoln in accepting the presents while courteously refusing the elephants. In a letter addressed to his "Great and Good Friend" Lincoln thanked the king for his gifts and explained that he could not personally keep them:

> Your majesty's letters show an understanding that

our laws forbid the President from receiving these rich presents as personal treasures. They are therefore accepted in accordance with Your Majesty's desire as tokens of your good will and friendship for the American People. . . .

[They] will be placed among the archives of the Government, where they will remain perpetually as tokens of mutual esteem. . . .

As for the proffered breeding stock, Lincoln wrote:

> I appreciate most highly Your Majesty's tender of . . . a stock from which a supply of elephants might be raised on our own soil. This Government would not hesitate to avail itself of so generous an offer if the object were one which could be made practically useful in the present condition of the United States. Our political jurisdiction, however, does not reach a latitude so low as to favor the multiplication of the elephant, and steam . . . has been our best and most efficient agent of transportation in internal commerce.

Each succeeding administration conducted its own search for precedents and an examination of the Presidential conscience in regard to foreign gifts. When the sultan of Turkey presented President Grover Cleveland with a jewel-encrusted medal to commemorate the four-hundredth anniversary of the discovery of America, the President sought the advice of the Department of State on the propriety of accepting it. Alvin A. Adee, Second Assistant Secretary of State, summarized a comprehensive review of pertinent legislation and precedent:

> While Congress has on many occasions authorized officers of the United States to accept presents from foreign governments, I do not find . . . any authority granted to the President to receive such present for himself.

The medal was accordingly placed in the collections of the Smithsonian Institution.

Some Presidents applied to themselves the rule established by Congress for American diplomats and military men that an officer was ineligible to take possession of gifts only while actually in office. When Calvin Coolidge left office in 1929, the State Department sent him eight medals, a shield, a photograph of the president of the Irish Free State, and two elephant tusks from among the things it had been holding for him until his retirement from office.

Still, no permanently satisfactory position on the matter developed. After the inauguration of Herbert Hoover the usual search for a policy took place. Between March 9 and May 9, 1929, eight opinions on the subject were offered from five offices in the Department of State: the solicitor (three memoranda), the Office of Coordination and Review, the Division of Western European Affairs, the Division of Protocol, and the assistant secretary. Assistant Secretary William E. Castle's final word betrayed a bit of irritation at such a teapot tempest: "It seems to me," he wrote, "that we might as well continue to act as reasonable individuals. . . . Nobody is going to bribe Mr. Hoover."

Finally President Franklin D. Roosevelt provided one practical solution to the problem of gifts from foreign governments when he originated the concept of a Presidential library. Principally established to house the President's papers and those of individuals closely associated with the President and his administration, the Roosevelt Library at Hyde Park, New York, is also the repository for many gifts of state. After the Harry S Truman Library was built in Independence, Missouri, former President Herbert Hoover decided that a similar arrangement in West Branch, Iowa, would facilitate the use of documents from his administration by scholars and the public. With the addition of the Dwight D. Eisenhower Library in Abilene, Kansas, the Lyndon B. Johnson Library in Austin, Texas, and the John F. Kennedy Library soon to be constructed in Cambridge, Massachusetts, there are now six libraries administered by the National Archives and Records Service of the General Services Administration. It has now become the custom for a President to place the gifts he receives while in office in the museum associated with his Presidential library. As the United States has assumed its position as a major world power the acceptance of gifts by the President has been increasingly taken for granted, and the Presidential library museums contain examples of the arts and crafts of nearly the entire world.

Although the receiving of official gifts caused endless diplomatic and ethical dilemmas, the giving of official presents never seems to have raised qualms in American minds. Some of the early gifts foreshadowed military-assistance programs of a later day. When the emperor of Morocco sought to buy a hundred gun carriages during the war between Tripoli and the United States in 1802, President Jefferson wrote to him that

> we feel it more conformable with our disposition to your majesty to ask your acceptance of them as a mark of the esteem and respect we bear you. . . .

And the pet lions forcibly presented to Consul Carr were sent in appreciation for a present of "two field pieces and ammunition."

Books were a favorite selection. In 1847 Secretary of State James Buchanan "caused to be handsomely bound and lettered" for presentation to the sultan of Turkey "the Indian Biographies of Hall & McKenney, and of Catlin." Other gifts were frequently described as "government publications." In the 1920's the Department of State kept on hand a supply of sets of Moore's *International Law Digest*. The first volume would be sent to the President with a suggested inscription for him to pen on the flyleaf before the books were sent off for presentation.

Photographs of the President were not released until all possible ramifications were explored. If it was thought that the possession of an autographed portrait could be used for political advantage or be construed as endorsement for a dubious cause, some other gift was chosen.

A rather strange decision was made in 1927 to send to the Empress Zauditu of Ethiopia a silver bowl purchased and engraved sixteen years earlier for presentation to her father, Emperor Menelik II. When a new American minister arrived at Addis Ababa in 1911 to present the bowl, he found that the emperor was too ill to receive him, and the bowl was returned to the Department of State. Before it was given to the Empress Zauditu, it received a thorough polishing and a new inscription. A note accompanied the bowl, explaining the origin of the gift.

In recent years Presidents have chosen a variety of presentation pieces. President Eisenhower often made gifts of fine Steuben glass. Among the presents of the Johnson administration were two interesting ones: a faithful reproduction of a wooden lap desk designed by Thomas Jefferson and a copy of an unusual brass candlestick that belonged to George Washington. Mrs. John F. Kennedy was inspired by the mineral collection at the Smithsonian Institution to have New York jeweler David Webb create a series of paperweights made of American minerals mounted in gold. One was made of New Mexican azurite and malachite in a mounting that resembled blades of grass with tiny gold and turquoise flowerettes; another was American topaz held by an American eagle executed in gold. President Nixon has taken advantage of the moon landings during his administration to prepare unique gifts for several heads of state. Tiny bits of moon rock were embedded in lucite on wooden bases. These were accompanied by a miniature of the recipient's national flag, which had made the trip to the moon and back.

On the whole, the trained Old World diplomat of the eighteenth or nineteenth century would be pained indeed to see the unglamorous settings of some modern diplomatic meetings, and the frequent disregard of traditional etiquette and courtesy might grieve him. He would find no consolation in the unadorned, functional bindings of many present-day international agreements. But his heart would rejoice when he learned that the President of the United States had at last come to view the exchange of gifts as a gracious gesture rather than attempted bribery. In this respect at least, the age of elegance has survived, and the American conscience has permitted the arts of diplomacy to flourish.

In her job as a member of the staff of the National Archives, Dr. Purdy arranged an exhibit on the "art" of diplomacy in 1971, and this article grew out of that exhibit. She was assisted in her research by her colleagues Dr. Edith James Blendon and the late Thomas M. Power.

our own members shared this and left the movement—that the cause of suffrage should be abandoned during wartime, that we should work instead for peace. But this was the same argument used during the Civil War, after which they wrote the word "male" into the Constitution. Did you know that "male" appears three times in the Fourteenth Amendment? Well, it does. So we agreed that suffrage came *before* war. Indeed, if we had universal suffrage throughout the world, we might not even have wars. So we continued picketing the White House, even though we were called traitors and pro-German and all that.

Mrs. *Irwin wrote in her book that on one occasion a sailor tried to steal your suffrage sash on the picket line and that you were dragged along the sidewalk and badly cut.*

Oh, no. She wrote *that*? No, that never happened. You know, when people become involved in a glorious cause, there is always a tendency, perhaps, to enlarge on the circumstances, to magnify situations and incidents.

And is there, perhaps, on your part a tendency to be overmodest about your activities?

I wouldn't know about that. All this seems so long ago and so unimportant now, I don't think you should be taking your precious lifetime over it. I try always, you know, to vanquish the past and try to be a new person.

But it is true, isn't it, that you were arrested outside the White House on October 20, 1917, and sentenced to seven months in the District of Columbia jail?

Yes.

And that when you were taken to the cell-block where the other suffragists were being held, you were so appalled by the stale air that you broke a window with a volume of Robert Browning's poetry you had brought along to read?

No. I think Florence Boeckel, our publicity girl, invented that business about the volume of Browning's poetry. What I actually broke the window with was a bowl I found in my cell.

Was this the reason you were transferred to solitary confinement in the jail's psychopathic ward?

I think the government's strategy was to discredit me. That

the other leaders of the Woman's Party would say, well, we had better sort of disown this crazy person. But they didn't.

During the next three or four weeks you maintained your hunger strike. Was this the second or third time you underwent forcible feeding?

Probably, but I'm not sure how many times.

Is this done with liquids poured through a tube put down through your mouth?

I think it was through the nose, if I remember right. And they didn't use the soft tubing that is available today.

While you were held in solitary confinement your own lawyer, Dudley Field Malone, could not get in to see you. And yet one day David Lawrence, the journalist, came in to interview you. How do you explain this?

I think he was a reporter at that time, but anyway he was a very great supporter of and, I guess, a personal friend of President Wilson's. I didn't know then what he was, except that he came in and said he had come to have an interview with me. Of course, a great many people thought that Lawrence, because of his close connection with the White House, had been encouraged to go and look into what the women were doing and why they were making all this trouble and so on.

You and all the other suffragist prisoners were released on November 27 and 28, just a few days after Lawrence's visit. Could this action have been based on his report to the President?

I wouldn't know about that. Of course, the only way we could be released would be by act of the President.

And on January 9, 1918, President Wilson formally declared for federal suffrage. The next day the House passed the amendment 274–136, and the really critical phase of the legislative struggle began.

Yes. Well, when we began, Maud Younger, our congressional chairman, got up this card catalogue, which is now on loan to the Library of Congress. We had little leaflets printed, and each person who interviewed a congressman would write a little report on where this or that man stood. We knew we had the task of winning them over, man by man, and it was important to know what our actual strength was in Congress at all times. These records showed how, with each Congress, we were getting stronger and stronger, until we finally thought we were at the point of putting the Anthony amendment to a vote. And of course this information was very helpful to our supporters in Congress.

Yet when the Senate finally voted on October 1, 1918, the amendment failed by two votes of the necessary two thirds. What happened?

We realized that we were going to lose a few days before the vote. We sat there in the Senate gallery, and they talked on and on and on, and finally Maud Younger and I went down to see what was going on, why they wouldn't vote. People from all over the country had come. The galleries were filled with suffragists. We went to see Senator Curtis, the Republican whip, and the Republican leader, Senator Gallinger. It was then a Republican Senate. And there they stood, each with a tally list in their hands. So we said, why don't you call the roll. And they said, well, Senator Borah has deserted us, he has decided to oppose the amendment, and there is no way on earth we can change his mind.

Y*ou thought Borah was on your side?*

Oh, yes. He wanted our support for his re-election campaign that year out in Idaho, and our organizer out there, Margaret Whittemore, had a statement signed by him that he would vote for the suffrage amendment. But then he changed. He never gave any reason for changing.

Did you then oppose him in the November election?

We opposed him, yes. We cut his majority, but he was re-elected, and from a suffrage state.

Was it about this time that your members began burning the President's statements in public?

I'm not sure when it started. We had a sort of perpetual flame going in an urn outside our headquarters in Lafayette Square. I think we used rags soaked in kerosene. It was really very dramatic, because when President Wilson went to Paris for the peace conference, he was always issuing some wonderful, idealistic statement that was impossible to reconcile with what he was doing at home. And we had an enormous bell—I don't recall how we ever got such an enormous bell—and every time Wilson would make one of these speeches, we would toll this great bell, and then somebody would go outside with the President's speech and, with great dignity, burn it in our little caldron. I remember that Senator Medill McCormick lived just down the street from us, and we were constantly getting phone calls from him saying they couldn't sleep or conduct social affairs because our bell was always tolling away.

You had better results from the next Congress, the Sixty-sixth, didn't you?

Yes. President Wilson made a magnificent speech calling for the amendment as a war measure back in October, 1918, and on May 20, 1919, the House passed the amendment. Then on June 4 the Senate finally passed it.

Did you go to hear the President?

I don't believe we were there, because when the President spoke, everybody wanted tickets, and the Woman's Party has never asked for tickets, because we still don't want to be in any way under any obligation. I know we were in the gallery when the Senate actually voted, because nobody wanted tickets then. Our main concern was that the Senate might try to reinstate the seven-year clause that had been defeated in the House.

The seven-year clause?

This clause required the amendment to be ratified by the states within seven years or else the amendment would be defeated. We got the clause eliminated on the suffrage amendment, but we were unable to stop Congress from attaching it to the present equal-rights amendment.

Were you relieved when the Anthony amendment finally passed?

Yes, for many reasons. But we still had to get it ratified. We went to work on that right away and worked continuously for the fourteen months it took. But that last state . . . we thought we never would get that last state. And, you know, President Wilson really got it for us. What happened was that Wilson went to the governor of Tennessee, who was a Democrat. The President asked him to call a special session of the state legislature so the amendment could be ratified in time for women to vote in the 1920 Presidential election.

That was on August 18, 1920, and there is a well-known photograph of you, on the balcony of your headquarters, unfurling the suffrage flag with thirty-six stars. What were your feelings that day?

You know, you are always so engrossed in the details that you probably don't have all the big and lofty thoughts you should be having. I think we had this anxiety about how we would pay all our bills at the end. So the first thing we did was to just do nothing. We closed our headquarters, stopped all our expenses, stopped publishing our weekly magazine, *The Suffragist*, stopped everything and started paying off the bills we had incurred. Maud Younger and I got the tiniest apartment we could get, and she took over the housekeeping, and we got a maid who came in, and we just devoted ourselves to raising this money.

What happened to Lucy Burns, your co-leader?

Well, she went back, I guess, to her home in Brooklyn. Everybody went back to their respective homes. Then the following year, on February 15, 1921, we had our final convention to decide what to do. Whether to disband or whether to continue and take up the whole equality program—equality for women in all fields of life—that had been spelled out at the Seneca Falls convention in•1848. We decided to go on, and we elected a whole new national board, with Elsie Hill as our new chairman. We thought we ought to get another amendment to the Constitution, so we went to many lawyers—I remember we paid one lawyer quite a large sum, for us, at least—and asked them to draw up an amendment for equal rights. We had another meeting up in Seneca Falls on the seventy-fifth anniversary of the original meeting, and there we adopted the program we have followed ever since on the equal-rights amendment. That was 1923. So that is when we started.

W*as that the year the first equal-rights amendment was introduced?*

We hadn't been able to get any lawyer to draft an amendment that satisfied us, so I drafted one in simple ordinary English, not knowing anything much about law, and we got it introduced in Congress. But at the first hearing our little group was the only one that supported it. All these other organizations of women that hadn't worked to get the vote, these professional groups and so on, opposed the amendment on the grounds that it would deprive them of alimony and force them to work in the mines, and they would lose these special labor laws that protect women. So it was obvious to us—and to the Congress—that we were going to have to change the thinking of American women first. So we began going to convention after convention of women, trying to get them to endorse E.R.A. It took many years. The American Association of University Women just endorsed it in 1972. Imagine, all the years and years and years that women have been going to universities. But the new generation of college women were so hopeless on this subject.

It was like forty years in the wilderness, wasn't it?

Yes, more or less. But during that time we opened—and by "we" I mean the whole women's movement—we opened a great many doors to women with the power of the vote, things like getting women into the diplomatic service. And don't forget we were successful in getting equality for women written into the charter of the United Nations in 1945.

Do you think the progress of the equal-rights amendment has been helped by the women's liberation movement?

I feel very strongly that if you are going to do anything, you have to take one thing and do it. You can't try lots and lots of reforms and get them all mixed up together. Now, I think the liberation movement has been a good thing, because it has aroused lots of women from their self-interest, and it has made everyone more aware of the inequalities that exist. But the ratification of the equal-rights amendment has been made a bit harder by these people who run around advocating, for instance, abortion. As far as I can see, E.R.A. has nothing whatsoever to do with abortion.

How did abortion become involved with equal rights?

At the 1968 Republican convention our representative went before the platform committee to present our request for a plank on equal rights, and as soon as she finished, up came one of the liberation ladies, a well-known feminist, who made a great speech on abortion. So then all the women on the platform committee said, well, we're not going to have the Republican Party campaigning for abortion. So they voted not to put *anything* in the party platform about women's rights. That was the first time since 1940 that we didn't get an equal-rights plank in the Republican platform. And then that feminist showed up at the Democratic convention, and the same thing happened with their platform. It was almost the same story at the 1972 conventions, but this time we managed to get equal rights back into the platforms.

I*t's really the principle of equal rights that you're concerned with, isn't it, not the specific applications?*

I have never doubted that equal rights was the right direction. Most reforms, most problems are complicated. But to me there is nothing complicated about ordinary equality. Which is a nice thing about our campaign. It really is true, at least to my mind, that only good will come to everybody with equality. If we get to the point where everyone has equality of opportunity—and I don't expect to see it, we have such a long, long way ahead of us—then it seems to me it is not our problem how women use their equality or how men use their equality.

Miss Paul, how would you describe your contribution to the struggle for women's rights?

I always feel . . . the movement is a sort of mosaic. Each of us puts in one little stone, and then you get a great mosaic at the end. ☆

Bourbon CONTINUED FROM PAGE 63

This article is adapted from a speech delivered before the Chicago Historical Society by Gerald Carson, author of The Social History of Bourbon *(Dodd, Mead & Company, 1963) and a frequent contributor to this magazine. Though he has often written about the eating and drinking habits of Americans, Mr. Carson professes no preference for any particular libation.*

say that making copper-distilled, sour-mash corn whiskey was a way of life among a pioneer people. This accounts for the vague background of Kentucky distilling and the highly imaginative stories about bourbon's origin.

Liquor and the evangelical churches once lived compatibly together. The minister's pay was often calculated in whiskey. Edward Eggleston refers in *The Hoosier Schoolmaster*, published in 1871, to a denomination known as Whiskey Baptists, and it is undoubtedly true that Saint Paul's admonition to Timothy—to "use a little wine for thy stomach's sake" (I Tim. 5:23)—was enthusiastically followed by many devout church members. The excesses of what may be called the Dark Age of American Drinking, climaxing somewhere around 1860, produced a new climate of opinion in which spirits were widely denounced as "The Serpent on the Sideboard."

The reasons for the heavy drinking can be understood from a human point of view. They lay in the cultural heritage of an Anglo-Saxon–Celtic ancestry, in a life of hardship and exposure, in a lack of social outlet. "Hot waters" were a fair substitute for the central heating that had not yet been invented and served to soften the rigors of Calvinistic religion.

Despite the deep feeling that existed in America against taxes on consumption, Congress passed an internal-revenue act in 1862 taxing domestic liquors to help finance the Civil War. Alcohol, not one of life's necessities, meets marvelously well the criteria for the art of taxation, which Jean Baptiste Colbert, celebrated finance minister to Louis XIV, described as consisting of "so plucking the goose as to procure the largest quantity of feathers with the least possible amount of squealing." The tax on alcohol disturbed an ancient way of life among the southern highlanders, where community opinion supported the practice celebrated in the old song:

> I'll go to some holler
> I'll put up my still
> I'll make you one gallon for a two
> dollar bill.

The moonshiner has usually been treated either humorously or romantically in popular literature. But these people were not comics or Robin Hoods. After a course in weaving chair bottoms in the state penitentiary they always went back to the mash rake and the meal vats. And sometimes there was the crack of a Winchester down in the hollow and a splash of blood on the laurel.

A revenue agent, so an old story goes, encountered a boy at the door of a mountainside shack.

"Is your father around, sonny?"

"Nope. Pap's up thar makin'."

"Makin'?"

"You know—'shine."

"Up where, did you say?"

"Yander," pointing toward the steep hillside.

"Is your mother at home?"

"Ma's up thar, too, helping pappy."

"Sonny," said the officer, "could you use fifty cents? All you have to do is to take me up there where I can talk to your father and mother."

Silently the boy held out his hand.

"No, no," the government man objected. "Not now, but later—after we get back."

"I'll take the money now," said the boy. "You ain't coming back."

Of all alcoholic potables the most majestic, ornamental, and ceremonial is the bourbon drink for great occasions—the mint julep. Its gentle sway has produced a lore that is vast, intricate, and controversial. There are sharp disputes about whether to crush or not to crush the mint or whether the use of alien liquors, such as Georgia corn whiskey sweetened with molasses, should be condoned. These are issues that have estranged and embittered the most devoted of friends. Take, for example, the anguish that the late Colonel Irvin S.

Cobb, a man who had a cigar, a bridge, a hotel, and a julep named after him, felt when he heard that his friend H. L. Mencken not only crushed the mint but poured Baltimore rye into his julep cup as well. Of this barbarity Cobb said: "Any guy who'd put rye in a mint julep and crush the leaves, would put scorpions in a baby's bed."

Kentuckians, who were offering silver julep-goblets as prizes at county fairs as long ago as 1816, have written with eloquence and poetic sentiment of their old bourbon that, as they say, "sits up in the glass," and they have described in loving detail the proper architecture of the julep. A realistic variation upon the lyric approach to this sensitive topic comes from the accomplished pen of the late, great editor Henry "Marse" Watterson of the Louisville *Courier-Journal*, who wrote:

Pluck the mint gently from its bed, just as the dew of the evening is about to form upon it. Select the choicer sprigs only, but do not rinse them. Prepare the simple syrup and measure out a half-tumbler of whiskey. Pour the whiskey into a well-frosted silver cup, *throw the other ingredients away and drink the whiskey.*

95

his own monumental *Handbook of American Indians, North of Mexico,* and by a foreword written for the first volume by President Roosevelt, who by then had become quite friendly with Curtis and had already employed him to take the photographs at the wedding of his daughter, Alice, to Nicholas Longworth.

The project, however, almost stopped there. Despite an appreciative reception from the subscribers and various newspapers that were apprised of the publication (the backing of the President and of Morgan, who donated nineteen of his twenty-five copies to libraries, made it a news event), Curtis still had only a small number of subscribers, not all of whom had yet paid him, and he could not meet publication costs for the next two volumes. Seattle banks had promised him loans, but the Panic of 1907 had occurred, and they had reneged. After spending another winter of uninterrupted work, this time in a log cabin in the Montana Rockies, preparing the text for Volumes III and IV, Curtis hurried to New York, desperate again. "Just how I pulled through, I do not know," he said. But mostly by persuading some of his wealthier subscribers to pay him in full he was able to get the next two volumes to press.

Still, the project's road was a bumpy one. Morgan's money financed the field work, but there was no guarantee that publication costs could continue to be met. In 1909, recognizing the problem, Morgan helped Curtis set up a corporation, The North American Indian, Inc., to handle the business details and meet the expenses of publishing the books. Then, in January, 1911, the original five-year agreement with Morgan for field money came to an end, and Curtis could not ask the financier to extend the grant. Save for a few weeks in the West he spent more than a year trying to find new subscribers whose payments would underwrite the field costs. At the end of June, 1912, he gave up the effort, and with what little money he had raised (principally, he said, through a second mortgage on his house), he rejoined his assistants in the field, "inadequately outfitted and short of funds to do efficient work."

The next year, with Volume IX on its way to press, the elder Morgan died in Europe, alarming Curtis that now his publication support would end. Fortunately the financier's son, J. P. Morgan the Younger, assumed his father's commitment, apparently even opening a line of credit for the publishing corporation at his bank. After that the project rolled more smoothly, with Curtis frequently able to hire large staffs to assist him with his photographic work, logistics, and research. Two volumes, with their portfolios, appeared in 1915 and 1916, and nine between 1922 and 1930, when Volume XX, the last one, was issued. Through the years Curtis continued to drive himself and his assistants, often working twenty hours a day for days at a

stretch. His last field trip, conducted principally in a forty-foot boat, was made in 1927 to Alaska, where he photographed Eskimo life for his final volume.

With the set finally completed, Curtis suffered a nervous breakdown and physical collapse. By 1932, however, he was recovered and lived another twenty years, turning his interest to other things, including an expedition to some mines in South America, occasional photographic projects, and the writing of several books. His great Indian volumes, stowed away in rare-book rooms, were almost entirely forgotten, and their magnificent photographs remained generally unknown. On October 21, 1952, at the age of eighty-four, Curtis died in Los Angeles, where he and his family had moved from Seattle.

In 1935, after a total of two hundred fourteen sets had been sold, a representative of the Morgan interests had meanwhile sold the assets of The North American Indian, Inc., to the Boston bookdealer and publisher Charles E. Lauriat for a thousand dollars plus royalties. Included were a small number of unsold sets, several thousand individual prints, unbound sheets, and the handmade copperplates from which the books and portfolios had been made. For some reason all of Curtis' original glass-plate negatives, which had been stored in a basement of the Pierpont Morgan Library in New York, were never shipped to Lauriat, and during World War II they were unwittingly dispersed. Some of them were destroyed, but many of them, sold as junk, ended up in the hands of collectors. In Boston, Lauriat found purchasers for the few sets he had acquired and then, from the unbound material, supplemented by material printed from the original plates, he assembled and sold fourteen more sets, bringing the total number of them marketed by Curtis and himself to two hundred seventy-two. From time to time private collectors and others showed an interest in buying the copperplates from Lauriat and bringing out a new, cheaper edition of Curtis' set. But always the costs proved too high, and potential purchasers of such a set would turn out to be scarce.

In the late 1950's, however, public interest in Indians began to revive, and researchers began to come on Curtis' books. Republication of several of his photographs in *The American Heritage Book of Indians* in 1961 was followed by the printing of more of his pictures in other publications and, finally, by the issuing of illustrated books devoted entirely to Curtis and his Indian photographs.

Today a new and exciting chapter in Curtis' saga is under way. Two years ago a group of investors in Santa Fe finally purchased all of Lauriat's remaining Curtis materials. Soon afterward they were joined by a group in Boston, headed by John A. Sodergren, a graduate student in anthropology at Harvard, and David Napior, who with Sodergren owns a small social-research firm in Cambridge. The two groups combined into a Massachusetts corporation of eleven individuals, using the old name, North American Indian, Inc., to take up the publishing of Curtis' books and prints where Curtis and Lauriat had left off.

Doing business as Curtis Gravures, the group has already sold a few complete sets, several individual volumes, and a number of the prints that came to them from Lauriat. But following the high standards set by Curtis—making prints by hand from the original copperplates on a flat-bed press and using the best paper, printing, and binding available—they plan to produce and sell two hundred twenty-eight new sets, matching those made by Curtis, and thus complete the 500-set edition originally planned.

In one of his interviews, when he was still busy with his project, Curtis was asked what Americans had made of the Indian—a question that he answered, ironically, in terms of what he had seen and come to feel but had taken great pains not to photograph. "We made of him," he replied, "a race totally discouraged. . . . Forced to the wall, with no escape, he has accepted his dull fate with the grim stoicism of his race, and has ceased to try to combat or avert it. Our efforts to extend assistance to him have been insincere and he has known it; linked, unwillingly, with cupidity and stupid lack of understanding, even the work of those few honest men who really tried to help him has been wasted— has been worse than wasted, for it has been harmful. We have always wronged the Indian but the greatest wrongs we are doing him today are born of our misunderstanding of him. The hardest of his manifold misfortunes came through the ever-changing policies by which we managed him after he had been fully conquered. We have ever been and still are vacillating and uncertain in our dealings with him. . . ."

Curtis' photographs have sometimes been criticized for showing none of the wrongs he saw. Although he photographed Indians when the authoritarian hand of government agents, of missionaries, and of soldiers lay heavily on the reservations and when the tribal peoples were enduring the period of their greatest suffering—many of them shorn of their leadership and traditional organizations, subjected to harsh punishments, denied freedoms, and often maintained at near-starvation levels—Curtis' idealized pictures give no hint of any of it. That, however, was not his goal as he originally expressed it to Grinnell in 1900 and as he carried it through to completion thirty years later.

Are they perversions of the truth or, at best, the fictional works of a romantic who paid Indians to show themselves, not as they were, but as he wanted them to be? Look closely into those faces. Even as they bore the oppression and misery that Curtis did not picture, they show the dignity and pride that defied and endured it. This, if anything, is the greatness of Curtis' Indian photographs. For all Americans, now and in the future, this is the way Curtis wanted us to remember them. ☆

ON TO SCHENECTADY! (*see cover*)

Thinking of the energy crisis, the poor, decrepit Penn Central Railroad, and the thin trickle of trains on Amtrak, we turn in this issue to a contrasting scene when railroading had all its future before it, the moment of departure for the first steam passenger train on the Mohawk & Hudson Railroad on August 9, 1831. Though it was not the very first scheduled train to be pulled by a locomotive (that was the *Best Friend of Charleston* on Christmas Day the year before), it was the second in America, and it was the best remembered, thanks to that fine genre painter Edward Lamson Henry, who created the huge canvas below, 42¾ × 110 inches in size. (Our cover is a detail.) The job was done in 1892-3, in time to be exhibited at the World's Columbian Exposition in Chicago in 1893.

Henry, like Norman Rockwell in our time, had an enormous insight into ordinary people and into homely, everyday life, and all his paintings will reward the onlooker who takes the pains to walk up and study the detail in them. He carefully investigated everything that went into *The First Train*. He bought books, and costumes, and even wagons for his task; he went to the site, a crossroads just two miles west of Albany, and talked to a few people who remembered the glorious day.

Pulled by the diminutive *DeWitt Clinton*—no bell, no whistle, no headlight, no brakes, no pilot wheels, not even a cab—three old stagecoaches mounted on flanged wheels

are filling up with a crowd. The engineer stokes his wood fire, and the conductor, trumpet in hand, runs along the train, making final arrangements. The usual detritus of railroading—stone ties, bunches of strap iron for the rails —is already apparent in the foreground. Inside or out, the passengers are expectant but apprehensive.

With only slack chains for couplings, it was a jerky trip: seventeen miles under a shower of sparks in a hundred and five minutes, but only thirty-eight racing back. The promoters and the president (the old patroon Stephen Van Rensselaer) were delighted. Within months dozens of new railroads were clamoring for charters; eventually the Mohawk & Hudson became part of the New York Central. For many years before its merger into the Penn Central, when the company was still strong and proud, a replica of the *DeWitt Clinton* and her little string of carriages stood in a place of honor at Grand Central Terminal in New York. Abandoned, like so much else, by the Penn Central, the engine is now at the Ford Museum in Dearborn, Michigan.

In a dream brought on by the energy crisis we see the museums and the tourist railroads disgorging their hundreds of ancient coal- and wood-burners and revitalizing the branch lines of the land, the old *DeWitt Clinton* chuffing proudly at their head. They work; no built-in obsolescence here. And the dream ends with a rousing, ironic toast to the men who made it possible, the sheiks of Araby. —O.J.

Reading, Writing, and History

THE DREAM AND THE DEAL:
The Federal Writers' Project 1935–1943
by Jerre Mangione
Little, Brown and Co. 416 pp. $12.50

"Out of this nettle, danger," says Hotspur in Shakespeare's *Henry IV,* Part I, "we pluck this flower, safety." The metaphor is so attractive that the urge to steal it is irresistible. So one notes, to begin with, that *The Dream and the Deal* is the story of how out of the nettle of economic catastrophe the nation plucked the flower of historical achievement. Told by Jerre Mangione, a novelist, eloquent nonfiction writer, and professor of English at the University of Pennsylvania, it is an account of the Federal Writers' Project of the Works Progress Administration. A make-work enterprise for jobless authors, the project turned into an unusual venture in exploring the American heritage—and the choice of words here is deliberate. The rollercoaster ride of the enterprise from crisis to crisis is a fascinating story in itself and an enlightening excursion into the workings of American culture, then and now.

The situation in April, 1935, was ugly. Between eight and ten million unemployed out of a labor force of some forty million. Dust storms and foreclosures on the farms, locked factory gates in the cities. A sodden

blanket of despair muffling the country's initiative toward recovery. Groping for palliatives as well as cures, Congress, under Presidential stimulus, passed the Emergency Relief Appropriation Act. Part of its effect was the creation of the Works Progress Administration, designed to give those on relief rolls work as well as handouts, in order to preserve their morale and their skills for a better day. In an unprecedented step WPA funding was supplied for four programs to employ those who worked in the fields of theatre, music, the fine arts, and writing. Unprecedented because the nation had no official cultural establishment, no tradition of government support for the arts, and a general distrust of those who did not earn a living in the "practical" world of farm, workshop, or office. But there were thousands of men and women whose work experience lay outside that world, and Congress seemed to agree with chief relief administrator Harry Hopkins' dictum: "Hell, they have to eat just like other people."

So the government stepped in to enable them to eat as well as they could on salaries of around twenty-three dollars a week. Their efforts, however, were not to be purely imaginative but were to have utilitarian objectives. The musicians and mummers of the Theatre and Music projects would entertain low-budget audiences. Members of the Art Project would decorate federal buildings [see "Memoirs of a WPA Painter," AMERICAN HERITAGE, October, 1970]. And the Writers' Project would reveal to tourists the terrain of America. Their initial assignment was the production of several regional travel guides, eventually to be synthesized into a single American guide. Time and chance altered this plan, and the one-volume American Baedeker never appeared under government auspices. What did emerge, however, was a collection of surprising variety.

By 1941 the total output of the Writers' Project included fifty-one major volumes, consisting of guides to every state, the District of Columbia, Puerto Rico, and Alaska, and also guides to several major cities. In addition, there were about a thousand

98

By BERNARD A. WEISBERGER

smaller books and pamphlets. There were mile-by-mile descriptions of three major roadways (*U.S. One, The Ocean Highway* from New Jersey to Florida, and *The Oregon Trail* from Missouri to the Pacific). There were a hundred and fifty volumes of a "Life in America" series that ranged in title from *Hands That Built New Hampshire* to *The Albanian Struggle in the Old World and the New.* There were short publications describing counties, small towns, and particular ethnic groups or occupations in various localities. There were collections of folktales and songs and pioneer reminiscences, and there were individual items as hard to classify as one simply entitled *Wisconsin Circus Lore.* Mangione includes a representative and intriguing sampling as an appendix.

Huge quantities of unpublished material collected by researchers still lie in various national, state, and local archives and libraries. It was gathered by a force of men and women numbering 6,686. The bulk of the work was completed in four years, and the total cost was some $27 million, about one fifth of one per cent of all appropriations for the WPA.

None of this was arrived at easily. The project was given into the care of Henry G. Alsberg, a fifty-seven-year-old former lawyer, playwright, reporter, and relief administrator. He had entertained youthful anarchist passions that by 1935 had cooled enough to make him acceptable to Congress, and he aged considerably in the four years of his tenure. For the problems of commanding an army of "writers, editors, historians, research workers, art critics, archaeologists, map draftsmen, geologists and other professional workers" under a federal bureaucracy were mountainous.

First there was staffing. Alsberg needed help in his Washington office, for his strong points of enthusiasm and high standards were offset by weaknesses that included too many cigarettes, an acid stomach (copiously dosed with Bisodol), and administrative sloppiness. He did get support from a competent headquarters team, of which Mangione became a member. But in the field he had to build a national organization consisting of a project director in each state, who would, unfortunately, be under the control of that state's WPA administrator. This latter functionary was, as often as not, a political appointee of no visible talent who meddled consistently with the project's work. And in some cases the project director himself was named at the "suggestion" of a senator or state boss, with disastrous consequences.

When Alsberg did find qualified project heads and local consultants, they were often, like all experts, resentful of direction from "outsiders" in Washington. So, from beginning to end, Alsberg's life was one of fairly continuous warfare with his subordinates, carried on by mail and telephone and interrupted by truces and treaties arranged through travelling trouble-shooters who were called field representatives. Work proceeded mostly in these lulls.

Next came the problems of writers and their special hang-ups. Never a calling to attract self-effacing conformists, literature has always had a high proportion of undisguised neurotics, alcoholics, and rascals of all kinds. Many had considerable competence but had to be carefully coddled into meeting schedules, as every editor knows—and "editor" Alsberg was kept unusually busy by his large collection of talent.

Unfortunately the talent was not universally distributed. Many project authors were, or would become, distinguished—among them, to name only a few, Saul Bellow, Nelson Algren, Richard Wright, Ralph Ellison, John Cheever, Kenneth Rexroth, and William Gibson. Of these, some worked hard on their project chores, and others stole the maximum feasible number of hours for their own creative work. Behind this phalanx of imaginative stars was a core of writers with solid academic or journalistic experience. But surrounding them was a sea of amateurs whose "writings" had never been published and who had nursed literary ambitions far beyond their skills in a variety of pre-Depression posts as teachers, administrators, and white-collar workers. Outside of major cities such as San Francisco, Chicago, and New York, where writers tended to concentrate, these untrained troops made up the bulk of the army. It was the task of the Washington office, then, to impose uniform quality on the output of this scattered array of poets, professors, hacks, drunks, civil servants, and aspirants to print.

And as a third headache there was the problem of left-wing politics. In a day when American maladies were obvious and urgent, and little was known about what actually went on in the Soviet Union, the panaceas of communism appealed to a number of writers with kind hearts, guilty consciences, and little experience with the realities of American life. The project was not allowed to inquire into the political background of applicants—a proviso inserted by Republicans to prevent favoritism to deserving Democrats. But the strategy backfired in allowing indeterminate numbers of Communists and fellow travellers to join the staff, in New York especially. There they conducted crusades against "right-wing" colleagues, intrigued against each other with a hatred that only Stalinists and Trotskyites seemed able to generate, and organized spectacular protests against cutbacks in staff. (The tactics of these protests included office sit-ins and the holding of administrators as prisoners.) There was no real evidence that Communists controlled the contents of the guidebooks in any way, but they impeded progress with their feuds, and, worse, they gave hostile congressmen a golden opportunity to denounce the arts projects in general and eventually to do them in.

By the spring of 1939, in fact, the project was in its last, fatal storm. Its strength had been sliced to thirty-five hundred staffers, and it was under heavy attack both from the House Appropriations Committee and from the Red-hunting Un-American Activities Committee of Representative Martin Dies. Roosevelt mounted no counteroffensive, and the reason was made clear to Mangione one warm May evening. A mutual friend of his and Mrs. Roosevelt's secured him an invitation to an informal Sunday White

House supper. Alsberg put his young assistant through a cram course in the project's accomplishments, hoping that it would all be conveyed to the Presidential ear. But the table topic dominating all others was the impending war in Europe and how the United States should prepare for it. Only after the President was wheeled from the room did Mangione get a chance to say a few words about the project to Mrs. Roosevelt. Her sentiments exhibited "the special kind of tenderness that people are likely to express for a dying friend." The era of social experimentation in Washington was ending; that of arming for conflict was at hand.

Soon afterward Alsberg was fired, and the project was given over to state control under the guidance of local sponsors. Publications continued to flow, but the unity of the enterprise was broken and its thematic strength sapped. Rechristened the Writers' Program, it was often made to serve the public-relations needs of various parochial interests. After Pearl Harbor its dwindling staff did writing chores for the armed services, and in 1943 they were absorbed into the Office of War Information. So the truly effective life of the project was only the four years from 1935 to 1939.

But the legacy is astonishing. Some 700,000 copies of the various guides have been sold to date, and there are collectors who rejoice with the passion of confirmed hobbyists in the possession of complete sets. Taken together, they form a compendium of information that sketches the social history of a kaleidoscopic nation. Each state guidebook consisted of an introductory set of essays on the history, geography, government, arts, architecture, education, recreation, local lore, and social features of the state. A second section described salient points of interest in a list of major cities. And a third, the largest, laid out highway tours to take. These, far from being prosaic rosters of mileages, accommodations, and mandatory sights to see, were made to bulge with as much miscellaneous information as the writers (who in most cases went over every mile of the ground themselves) could manage. Local feelings were neither flattered nor spared, and the only restraints observed, other than those of space, were provided by researchers and checkers who remorselessly kept the writers from soaring into undocumented flights of prose.

The essays are uneven in quality, though the best are superb. Many are now dated, but some states have issued new and revised versions that repair the damage of time to facts and statistics. Best of all are the tours, which offer still, in Bernard DeVoto's words, "a rich, various and rewarding spectacle." They have, as another reviewer noted, "the profuse disorder of nature and life" that "gets in your blood and sends you crowing from oddity to anecdote, from curiosity to dazzling illumination of single fact." Mangione presents an intriguing sampling; and to check matters further this reviewer picked up the books for New York, California, Texas, and Vermont, opened each at random, and unearthed the following representative facts before forcing himself back to the typewriter:

—The Beekman Arms Hotel, in Rhinebeck, New York, once had a sign in its office giving the rates as follows:
  Lodging 3 pence
  With breakfast, 4 pence
  Only 5 lodgers to a bed
  No boots can be worn in bed.

—In Oakland stands the home of the California poet Joaquin Miller. "The poet claimed he could not write without rain on the roof; he had pipes installed to sprinkle water on the roof when he wanted inspiration."

—In Texas, according to a 1969 revision of the original guide, coyotes still venture into the streets of small towns at night; a herd of buffalo is still maintained on the Goodnight ranch, the remnant of a herd of *sixty million* that once roamed the state; and wild turkeys are still plentiful in some sections.

—Bellows Falls, Vermont, on the Connecticut River, has a fifty-foot drop. Yet at least a dozen persons have gone over the edge and lived. The first was an Abnaki squaw, in 1781. "Carelessly allowing her canoe to be drawn to a point where she could not paddle against the current, the squaw drank a bottle of rum that she was taking to her brave and lay down in the canoe to await her fate. She was fished out below the falls, quite safe and quite drunk."

And one browses on, helplessly, through tales of freak storms, bad men and good, curious houses, vanished communities and trades, obscure and famous battles, unsung inventors, and dastardly crimes, all of which left their marks on the land. The richness of printed lore parallels the graphic feast spread for consumption in the Art Project's *Index of American Design.* [See AMERICAN HERITAGE, February and April, 1972.]

Like any massive undertaking, of course, the project's publications are not without fault. But the sum total was and is a composite portrait of what the critic Alfred Kazin called "an America unexampled in density and regional diversity." And this was done, not only in the midst of "capitalist America's" predicted doom, but just after the twenties, when a number of intellectuals had condemned their native land as a cultural wasteland, empty and crackling in the chill of "Puritan repression." The Writers' Project, under adverse circumstances, had helped a nation to discover and appreciate its true identity.

There is occasion for cheer in this story. We live in another kind of hard times, when pessimism is not easy to avoid. It takes an effort to remember that the United States—its land, its people, its institutions—adds up to something bigger than one generation's troubles and mistakes. It often takes an effort nowadays to remind ourselves that this country is sometimes better than its leaders, always more interesting than its image makers know, and durable enough to outlast the rhetoric of both its critics and its uncritical defenders. But Mangione is really telling us that we were in deep trouble before, and we almost accidentally paid for a self-portrait, and we liked and were strengthened by what we saw. ☆

POSTSCRIPTS TO HISTORY

HISTORY VERSUS HISTORICAL FICTION

The article about Nat Turner's rebellion in our October, 1973, issue ("Children of Darkness," by Stephen B. Oates) evoked this interesting comment from William Styron, the eminent author of the novel *The Confessions of Nat Turner:*

I think that the article covers the ground quite lucidly and comprehensively, and shows that Professor Oates has read the available source material well. It also demonstrates that while we can unearth a multitude of fascinating "facts" about the insurrection, the man himself and his deeper motivations remain, as with so many obscure historical figures, a matter of conjecture—hence the impulse to write plays about them, or novels, which should never even pretend to absolute "accuracy" even if accuracy were possible.

Although I have never heard of Professor Oates, he is a professional historian and I am not; therefore under ordinary circumstances I suppose I should be rattled that he should consider my fictional treatment of the rebellion "unacceptable." But other historians, vastly more eminent than Professor Oates and certainly more sophisticated in their understanding of the differences between fiction and history— I am thinking of C. Vann Woodward, Eugene Genovese and Martin Duberman —have all publicly testified to the historical integrity in my vision of Nat Turner. So I rest easy.

In any case, I am pleased that Professor Oates seems to be so happily engaged in the cottage industry I established up at the University of Massachusetts and elsewhere.

SAVING THE FACTORIES

We have just received word of a vigorous historic preservation society that was hitherto unknown to us. The Society for Industrial Archeology, which operates under the aegis of the National Museum of History and Technology in the Smithsonian Institution, is dedicated to the saving and refurbishing of monuments from our technological past. The society casts a wide net and addresses its attentions to such diverse relics as factories, railroad sheds, ferryboats, and canals. While constantly battling the problems of a "bad image" (factories are big and dirty and frequently viewed as symbols of exploitation), the society seems to be making good headway in its various campaigns.

A recent issue of the SIA newsletter reports with happy surprise that the C&O/B&O (combined) Railroad has announced a million-dollar renovation of the magnificent old B&O Museum in Baltimore, which houses in a huge circular 1884 car shop the finest collection of historical locomotives and rolling stock in the country. On the other hand, nobody was able to save the passenger shed of Chattanooga Union Depot, that city's last pre-Civil War building. The newsletter remarks that by and large, Chattanooga has been sadly indifferent to its historical heritage, industrial and otherwise. The city has no historical museum and the entire old part of town has been leveled. Little effort seems to have been made to explore adaptive uses for Union Depot although the preservation of the Southern's Terminal Station as *The Chattanooga Choo Choo* is commendable, despite its branding with a cutsie name.

The society, realizing that few industrial buildings are likely to be saved for their architectural purity alone, stresses adaptive use of surviving structures. For instance, the newsletter reports the old V M Ybor Cigar Factory complex in Tampa, Florida, is in the process of being transformed into a shopping mall with accommodations for apartments and museums above the shops. One wing, however, will be preserved as a cigar museum complete with artisans rolling cigars. Feather fanciers will rejoice in the salvation of a San Francisco feather factory that, with its basement feather-cleaning plant and three stories, will become a hardware store.

Perhaps the most startling adaptive-use proposal concerns our dwindling supply of Liberty Ships. Of the twenty-seven hundred built to carry goods during World War II something over one hundred survive today. About forty of these are in foreign cargo service, and seventy-two are mouldering in the moth-ball fleet and due for scrapping. One, however, may escape this fate. The *John W. Brown,* which has been serving as a floating school in New York City and is now due for replacement and return to the government, may be preserved as a floating marine museum.

We heartily endorse all of these projects and wish the Society for Industrial Archeology all good fortune in its efforts to preserve a most significant part of our past.

TALKING BOOKS

We are pleased to announce that AMERICAN HERITAGE has been selected by the Library of Congress to be reproduced on "Talking Books" and distributed by regional libraries throughout the United States to those whose handicaps would otherwise prevent them from reading the magazine. A statement to this effect appears on the title page of this issue and will continue to appear in future issues.

THE CALL TO GREATER DUTY

When, in 1917, America threw in her lot with the allied nations fighting against Germany, there was a national draft for the second time in our history. On the whole, Americans were enthusiastic about the crusade, but few can have been so forthright about their reasons as the mountain woman who wrote the letter that appears below. This unusual document was recently discovered among the Woodrow Wilson papers in the Library of Congress by Donald Smythe, an associate professor of history at John Carroll University.

Dear U.S.
  He can't rote.
  My husband ast for me to rote for him a recoment that he supports his family—he

ant done nothing but drink lemon essence and play the fiddle since I maried him 8 years ago—and I gotta feed seven kids of hisn. Take him away and welcome, for I need the grub and his bed for the kids. May bee you can get him to cary a gun for hes good on squirrels and eating.

Dont tell him, but take him.

Name Withheld

IN MY MERRY REO

Mr. Charles E. Hulse, an automotive historian who specializes in early Oldsmobiles, has written to call our attention to an error in a picture caption for the article about William C. Durant that appeared in our August, 1973, issue. Mr. Hulse writes:

I would disagree with the identification of the photo in the upper right-hand corner on page thirteen. This auto is not an Oldsmobile but a R.E.O., of 1905 or 1906 period. The man seated behind the wheel is not R. E. Olds. In fact, I fail to find Mr. Olds in the photo. I would identify the man behind the wheel as Mr. H. T. Thomas, a R.E.O. official.

OBSERVATIONS OF AN "AMATEUR" HISTORIAN

Don Russell, who has written extensively on the history of the American West, recently published an autobiographical essay entitled "How I Got This Way" in *The Western Historical Quarterly.* In it he traces his growth as a historian and makes some interesting observations on the study and uses of history. Herewith some excerpts.

It may be deduced . . . that I resent the tag "amateur," even though it does mean love of the subject. History is produced by professional writers and by professional teachers. That professors of history should arrogate to themselves the title of professional historian seems inequitable. Some of the most readable history that I have found was written by professors of English. Is a prejudice detectable here? From what I read in the newspapers and in books that should have remained Ph.D. theses, I might suspect a taint. However, one thing I have learned from historical research: Never make hasty (or any) generalizations. And I have never met a history professor I did not like.

. . . Have I learned anything from all this? Yes, to be skeptical of anything that is said, or written, and, above all, printed in type, to be suspicious of any idea on which historians are generally agreed, especially if it be in accord with the latest fad in scholarship. Repetition in type does not make truth of an original error. On the other hand, the historian, unlike the lawyer, cannot impeach a witness for one erroneous statement. Even if the witness is 90 percent wrong, the remaining 10 percent may have historical significance. Fact erodes as the square of the time elapsed since the action, but reminiscence still has its value, if only in recapturing the attitudes and emotions of an earlier day. Sometimes it gets down to just plain common sense: What is the most reasonable interpretation of conflicting testimony? Rarely will witnesses agree, but a deliberate lie is also uncommon.

I am intolerant of those who pass on as legends the lies they are too lazy to investigate; of writers who rush into print ignorant of their subject; of pedants who prove their lack of prejudice against popular minorities by exhibiting their prejudice against the majority; of hasty generalizing that condemns the army, the Indian Bureau, or the Establishment without understanding that all organized groups consist of individuals, some good, some bad, but mostly both; of explaining all failures by blaming a Custer, a Reno, a Lyndon Johnson, or some other historic character without considering that these were human beings, conditioned by their background of experience and personal characteristics to act the way they did and lacking our overwhelming advantage of hindsight; and of those who pervert their findings to fit a thesis.

History's enduring value lies in the interpretation of the present from the past. It loses all its values when we try to interpret the past from the present.

WHEN WE HAD MEAT TO SPARE

David Lowe, a frequent contributor to these pages, has come across an ebullient celebration of America's little-known part in bulwarking the British Empire.

In the 1870's and 1880's Chicago's meat-packers finally perfected methods of canning beef and thereby opened up vast new markets abroad. Among their best customers were European governments with armies and navies in tropical countries. England, in particular, was a steady and enthusiastic purchaser of the new product. To supply the 1884 expedition sent to crush a self-proclaimed prophet called the Mahdi, who was leading a revolt against British rule in the Sudan, Her Majesty's government ordered no less than 2,500,000 pounds of tinned provisions. (The campaign is remembered now chiefly because of the death of General "Chinese" Gordon at Khartoum.) This dependence of beef-loving England upon American stockyards inspired an anonymous Chicago rhymester to celebrate the fact in verse. "P.D.A." is, of course, Philip Danforth Armour; "W.E.G." is the British Prime Minister, William Ewart Gladstone; and the "Mackay-Bennett line" refers to the Commercial Cable Company organized in 1883 by John William Mackay and James Gordon Bennett.

The roast beef of old England
Is famed in song and story
Without it where was English brawn
That won old England glory?
But in these days of England's gloom,
When war's dread notes alarm her,
What does she send to save Khartoum?
Corned beef canned by Phil Armour.

When Gladstone first resolved on war,
No lack of ammunition
Delayed the movement up the Nile,
The problem was nutrition.
"Our cannonade," the Premier said,
"Must needs be sharp and brief,
Our cannonade, therefore shall be
Phil Armour's canned corned beef."

"To P.D.A.; Send p.d. quick,
Care John Bull, London docks,
Two million pounds of canned corned beef,
Ox tongues, pig's feet and hocks."
"To W.E.G.: (Send C.O.D.)"
Swift flashed the ready answer,
Wired per Mackay-Bennett line,
"I will, because I can, sir."

At every mile along the line
Fanatics like El Mahdi
Will soon be skirmishing to find
A soul to fit a body.
The prophet had a host of Khans,
And some were brave and able;
But then, you see, they couldn't win—
They lacked the Armour label.

AMERICAN HERITAGE SOCIETY TOURS

Anybody who is even marginally interested in American history has probably had the experience of setting out optimistically to visit a historic site and, after a forty-minute drive, being confronted by a forlorn and obscure huddle of earthworks. There may or may not be a rusted iron plaque explaining the works; if there is, it most likely reads something like "Fort Walworth, built in 1810, was the scene of severe fighting during Pierce's expedition of 1813. This marker erected and dedicated by the Daughters of the American Revolution, Newcomb Chapter, 1912." Armed with this meager information, the visitor can do little but prowl bleakly through a scattering of masonry and return, highly unsatisfied, to his hotel.

On the other hand, in a city such as Philadelphia the tourist can find himself facing such a baffling variety of historic monuments that he spends a confusing and unrewarding day battling for parking spaces and running through crowded restorations.

Recently the American Heritage Society, in hopes of giving its members better access to the American past, established a series of tours of historic America. The tours were an immediate success and are now beginning their fourth season. Each of the tours is a seven-day excursion through a historically interesting region of the country. The tour groups are kept small—twenty-five people at most—and the society has gone to great pains to ensure the finest special attention, meals, and accommodations available along the way. The groups are met by historians who conduct them through museums, restorations, and battlefields, as well as homes and private collections that are not open to the general public. Here is a list and brief description of the tours we are offering during 1974. They all begin on a Saturday and end where they started on Saturday a week later, with the exception of the Pennsylvania tour, which ends in Wilmington, Delaware.

Virginia May 11

We cover the formidable amount of history in this state with a tour that includes the twice-disputed battlefield at Bull Run; Jefferson's estate, Monticello; the city of Richmond; the scrupulously restored colonial city of Williamsburg; the city of Fredericksburg; and Gunston Hall Plantation.

California May 18

This journey through the northern part of the state begins in San Francisco and includes the once-notorious Barbary Coast; Muir Woods with its towering redwood trees; the Sonoma wine country; Sutter's Mill, where gold was discovered in 1848; Carmel-by-the-Sea; and San Simeon, the astonishing pleasure dome of the late William Randolph Hearst.

Pennsylvania June 8

Starting in Philadelphia, the tour covers Independence Square and Fairmount Park; Valley Forge, where Washington held his army together for a miserable winter; the rich Amish country; the magnificently preserved battlefield at Gettysburg; Brandywine River Museum, with its fine collection of Wyeth paintings; and the Winterthur Museum, with the finest collection of American furniture and decorations extant.

Northern New England September 28

From Boston the tour heads north to take in the splendid Federal-style shipowners' homes in Newburyport and goes on to visit the site of the original Portsmouth settlement at Strawbery Banke; the White Mountains, with their flaming fall foliage; Dartmouth College; the forty-five-acre Shelburne Museum; Fort Ticonderoga; the battlefield at Bennington; and the Hancock Shaker Village.

New York October 5

After a reception in New York City the tour heads up along the Hudson, stopping at the restored Adam-style mansion Boscobel; Franklin D. Roosevelt's home at Hyde Park; Olana, artist Frederick Church's Moorish fantasy of a house; Cooperstown, on Lake Otsego, James Fenimore Cooper's "Lake Glimmerglass"; Schenectady's eighteenth-century Village-Stockade; the fortress and military academy West Point; and Sleepy Hollow, made part of history and legend by Washington Irving.

New England Coast October 12

The tour leaves from Boston and includes stops at the Old North Church; Lexington and Concord, where the Revolution began; Sturbridge Village; the lovely restored colonial town of Old Deerfield; the Connecticut River Valley; Mystic Seaport whaling village; Newport, with its opulent "summer cottages"; New Bedford; and the meticulously reconstructed Plimoth Plantation.

For those who want to trace American history back to its British wellsprings, the society is offering three-week tours of England and Scotland. The tour of Scotland, which starts on June 5, will travel the highlands and lowlands of that kingdom. Included among the sights are castles and ruined abbeys; Loch Lomond; Culloden Moor, where English troops under "Butcher Cumberland" crushed the rebellion of Bonnie Prince Charlie; the Glen Grant distillery, where the tour will have a chance to taste thirty-year-old whisky straight from the wood; Inverness; Forres heath, where Macbeth met three witches; a textile mill; the beautiful Isle of Skye; Glasgow; and Edinburgh.

The tour of southern England starts at Winchester on October 3 and goes on to cover a vast amount of the Sceptered Isle. Included in the itinerary are stops at rustic inns and great houses; the ancient Roman city of Bath; the rugged Cornwall coast; the famous sea wall at Lyme Regis; the Royal Yacht Squadron; H.M.S. *Victory*, the mammoth three decker that Nelson commanded at Cape Trafalgar; Brighton, with its fantastic Royal Pavilion and its Victorian amusement piers; Canterbury; and, of course, London.

We are pleased to announce that some of our society members have returned to take as many as a half dozen tours. If you are interested in accompanying one of the above tours and want further information, please write Mrs. Audre Proctor, Reservations Manager, American Heritage, 1221 Avenue of the Americas, New York, N.Y. 10020, or telephone (212) 997-4789.

A Letter from Lord Macaulay

Because he had access to manuscripts that later were widely scattered, Henry Stephens Randall's Life of Thomas Jefferson *remained for nearly a century the most detailed account of America's third President. Randall, an educator and agriculturist with a predilection for politics and political history, was an ardent Jeffersonian Democrat. Soon after completing his estimable study he sent a copy to Thomas Babington Macaulay, the distinguished English author and former member of Parliament. Here is a portion of Lord Macaulay's response.*

Holly Lodge, Kensington,
London, May 23d, 1857.

Dear Sir,

. . . I have long been convinced that institutions purely democratic must, sooner or later, destroy liberty, or civilization, or both. In Europe, where the population is dense, the effect of such institutions would be almost instantaneous. What happened lately in France is an example. In 1848 a pure democracy was established there. During a short time there was reason to expect a general spoliation, a national bankruptcy, a new partition of the soil, a maximum of prices, a ruinous load of taxation laid on the rich for the purpose of supporting the poor in idleness. Such a system would, in twenty years, have made France as poor and barbarous as the France of the Carlovingians. Happily, the danger was averted; and now there is a despotism, a silent tribune, an enslaved press. Liberty is gone, but civilization has been saved. I have not the smallest doubt that if we had a purely democratic government here the effect would be the same. Either the poor would plunder the rich, and civilization would perish; or order and prosperity would be saved by a strong military government, and liberty would perish. You may think that your country enjoys an exemption from these evils. I will frankly own to you that I am of a very different opinion. Your fate I believe to be certain, though it is deferred by a physical cause. As long as you have a boundless extent of fertile and unoccupied land, your laboring population will be far more at ease than the laboring population of the Old World, and, while that is the case, the Jefferson politics may continue to exist without causing any fatal calamity. But the time will come when New England will be as thickly peopled as old England. Wages will be as low, and will fluctuate as much with you as with us. You will have your Manchesters and Birminghams, and in those Manchesters and Birminghams hundreds of thousands of artisans will assuredly be sometimes out of work. Then your institutions will be fairly brought to the test. Distress everywhere makes the laborer mutinous and discontented, and inclines him to listen with eagerness to agitators who tell him that is a monstrous iniquity that one man should have a million, while another can not get a full meal. In bad years there is plenty of grumbling here, and sometimes a little rioting. But it matters little. For here the sufferers are not the rulers. The supreme power is in the hands of a class, numerous indeed, but select; of an educated class; of a class which is, and knows itself to be, deeply interested in the security of property and the maintenance of order. Accordingly, the malcontents are firmly yet gently restrained. The bad time is got over without robbing the wealthy to relieve the indigent. The springs of national prosperity soon begin to flow again: work is plentiful, wages rise, and all is tranquillity and cheerfulness. I have seen England pass three or four times through such critical seasons as I have described. Through such seasons the United States will have to pass in the course of the next century, if not of this. How will you pass through them? I heartily wish you a good deliverance. But my reason and my wishes are at war, and I can not help foreboding the worst. It is quite plain that your Government will never be able to restrain a distressed and discontented majority. For with you the majority is the Government, and has the rich, who are always a minority, absolutely at its mercy. The day will come when, in the State of New York, a multitude of people, none of whom has had more than half a breakfast, or expects to have more than half a dinner, will choose a Legislature. Is it possible to doubt what sort of a Legislature will be chosen? On one side is a statesman preaching patience, respect for vested rights, strict observance of public faith. On the other is a demagogue ranting about the tyranny of capitalists and usurers, and asking why any body should be permitted to drink Champagne and to ride in a carriage, while thousands of honest folks are in want of necessaries. Which of the two candidates is likely to be preferred by a working-man who hears his children cry for more bread? I seriously apprehend that you will, in some such season of adversity as I have described, do things which will prevent prosperity from returning; that you will act like people who should in a year of scarcity devour all the seed-corn, and thus make the next a year not of scarcity, but of absolute famine. There will be, I fear, spoliation. The spoliation will increase the distress. The distress will produce fresh spoliation. There is nothing to stop you. Your Constitution is all sail and no anchor. As I said before, when a society has entered on this downward progress, either civilization or liberty must perish. Either some Cæsar or Napoleon will seize the reins of government with a strong hand, or your republic will be as fearfully plundered and laid waste by barbarians in the twentieth century as the Roman Empire was in the fifth; with this difference, that the Huns and Vandals who ravaged the Roman Empire came from without, and that your Huns and Vandals will have been engendered within your own country by your own institutions. . . .

I have the honor to be, dear sir, your faithful servant,

T. B. Macaulay

H. S. Randall, Esq., etc., etc., etc.